Food,
Foreign Policy,
and
Raw Materials
Cartels

Food, Foreign Policy, *and* Raw Materials Cartels

William Schneider

PUBLISHED BY

**Crane, Russak &
Company, Inc.**

NEW YORK

National Strategy
Information Center, Inc.

**Food, Foreign Policy,
and Raw Materials Cartels**

Published in the United States by

Crane, Russak & Company, Inc.

347 Madison Avenue
New York, N.Y. 10017

Library Edition: ISBN 0-8448-0921-7
Paperbound Edition: ISBN 0-8448-0922-5
LC 76-492

Strategy Paper No. 28

Printed in the United States of America

Table of Contents

Preface

Since the mid-1950s, economic warfare as an instrument of policy has had few proponents; and now, in another era of detente, the topic is almost taboo. Confidence in the efficacy of embargos and related measures was eroded by their alleged ineffectiveness against the Soviet bloc during the preceding decade; although a minority view still holds that Moscow's palpable craving for Western technology and capital implies that the previous policy of denial did, in fact, impair the Commissar-industrial complex at levels where the shroud of state secrecy could conceal weakness. More recently, interest in the concept of economic warfare has been revived by the Arab oil embargo imposed in the wake of the 1973 Yom Kippur War. In this instance, a 9.3 percent reduction in the flow of oil from the Persian Gulf area forced perceptible changes in the policies of the United States and its allies toward the belligerents in the Middle East conflict.

It is perhaps inevitable that others who control the sources of strategic raw materials will not long be indifferent to the lesson derived from the success of the Arab oil weapon. Already, Jamaica has quintupled the price of its bauxite, mined mostly by American companies. At the recent special conference of the UN, there was much discussion by Third World leaders of the possible need for new producers cartels, similar to OPEC, which could manipulate the prices of vital minerals as a way of influencing US policy. In view of these ominous trends, it seems timely to reexamine America's non-military options if other nations persist in wielding the instrument of economic warfare against us. (Although this seems an unlikely contingency, it should be noted that, despite Moscow summit meetings, Soviet propaganda is almost continually inciting the Arab world to use both oil cut-offs and investment fund shifts to cripple Western "imperialism.")

In his thoughtful analysis of this complex problem, Dr. William Schneider points out that, in the past, we have established an unrealistically high set of expectations for the results of economic warfare. This has colored the perspective of many policymakers as to what might reasonably be achieved by such techniques. Viewed more realistically, economic warfare can have a substantial impact on resource allocation in a developed economy such as the Soviet Union, and can pose a strong stimulus to agreement in a bargaining situation with an underdeveloped country.

Moreover, the United States is in a commanding position to conduct economic warfare in its own defense if the initiative of others propels us toward that distasteful option. American dominance of the agricultural export market is greater than Arab dominance of the petroleum market. Foreign demand for US agricultural products seems likely to increase indefinitely. Hence, the author suggests, the United States itself has an energy resource to support our diplomacy in its worldwide dealings with the Communist bloc countries and with the emerging nations of the Third World. (It is self-evident that all of our humanitarian instincts argue against resort to the "food weapon" in most conceivable situations. Yet it is also clear that, in an interdependent world, the industrialized West could not be passive if adversaries sought to orchestrate raw materials embargos that would generate mass unemployment and large-scale depression among the democracies. Who can foresee what emotional pressures for the return to gunboat diplomacy might be loosed if ten million Americans were out of work for lack of fuel and raw materials necessary to industry? Instead of running the risk of overreacting to blackmail, it is probably more "humane" to be candid in letting potential rivals know in advance that we are not without means to defend our position short of military conflict. As others have noted in the nuclear context, to talk and think about the "unthinkable" may go a long way toward inhibiting those who might be tempted to bring it to pass.)

Dr. Schneider, who is now Legislative Assistant to US Senator James L. Buckley of New York, received his B.S. degree from Villanova University, and his Ph.D. (in economics) from New York University. Prior to joining Senator Buckley's staff in January 1971, he was a member of the professional staff of the Hudson Institute.

He is coauthor and coeditor (with J. J. Holst) of *Why ABM? Policy Issues in the Missile Defense Controversy*, and has contributed numerous articles on economic and national security policy issues to various professional journals.

Preface to This Edition

Much of the material in this essay was published in July 1974 under the title, *Can We Avert Economic Warfare in Raw Materials? US Agriculture as a Blue Chip*, in NSIC's Agenda Papers series. Since then, developments have moved with such speed that an updated review of the character of US diplomatic leverage in the context of supply interruptions of raw materials has become necessary. During the past two years, nations producing exportable quantities of various raw materials including iron ore, bauxite, phosphate rock, and several other commodities have sought to emulate the success of the Organization of Petroleum Exporting Countries (OPEC) in increasing revenues through a combination of supply restrictions and price increases. These attempts have taken a number of forms, including taxation, direct government participation in foreign raw material investment, and nationalization.

This revised, updated, and much-expanded edition of the original publication reviews more extensively the lessons of the 1973-74 Arab oil embargo, and also the economic warfare experience in Chile in 1973. In addition, US vulnerabilities to raw material supply interruptions, particularly raw material supplies important for national security purposes, are evaluated. The discussion of US potential for agricultural exports has also been expanded to include supply and demand projections through 1985; and US assets and liabilities in the struggle to secure international economic policy objectives over the next decade are discussed at some length. Finally, two appendices have been added to include some important documentary material, including recent statements of US policy with respect to raw materials and agricultural exports.

Frank R. Barnett, *President*
National Strategy Information Center, Inc.

February 1976

1

Introduction

For some time, economic warfare has been out of fashion with US policymakers as a meaningful instrument of national policy. There was strong academic interest in the subject during World War II and the Korean War, but little serious research has been done since then.[1] The United States has had statutes in force ever since the Trading With the Enemy Act of 1917 to provide a legal basis for the conduct of economic warfare. But in recent years, specialists and policy-makers alike have been disenchanted with the efficacy of such measures to support foreign policy objectives against substantial adversaries. As a consequence, most of the economic warfare measures instituted since World War II, which have been directed primarily against the Soviet bloc, have not been energetically enforced. With the exception of some of the most sensitive military technology, little effort has been made to prevent leaks of important civilian technology to the Soviet bloc. Nor is there a significant consensus among policymakers as to how (if at all) economic warfare should be conducted in the future as an element of national policy against actual or potential adversaries.

The Arab oil embargo imposed on the United States and other nations in October 1973 has, however, stimulated a reconsideration

---

[1] For useful discussions of economic warfare, see R. L. Allen, *Soviet Economic Warfare* (Washington: Public Affairs Press, 1960); H. S. Ellis, *Exchange Control in Central Europe*, Harvard Economic Studies No. 69 (Cambridge: Harvard University Press, 1941); A. O. Hirschmann, *National Power and the Structure of Foreign Trade* (Los Angeles: University of California Press, 1945); J. Viner, *Dumping, A Problem of International Trade* (Chicago: University of Chicago Press, 1923); Y. Wu, *Economic Warfare* (Englewood Cliffs: Prentice-Hall, 1952) and Gunnar Adler-Karlsson, *Western Economic Warfare, 1947-1967*, (Stockholm: Almquist and Wiksell, 1968). A useful review of the development of the subject can be found in the *International Encyclopedia of the Social Sciences*, p. 467.

of the utility of resource control as a means of influencing international diplomatic behavior.

Postwar economic and monetary arrangements (Bretton Woods and GATT) were designed to support an economically interdependent world. This system has been based upon the notion—developed in over a century of economic thought—that free international commerce would inhibit military competition among the nations, and at the same time enhance their economic welfare. The 19th century economist and philosopher John Stuart Mill observed:[2]

> It is commerce which is rapidly rendering war obsolete by strengthening and multiplying the personal interests which are in natural opposition to it.

The higher economic standard of living which has been the result of the international specialization of labor in an environment of the free international movement of economic resources has become one of the most conspicuous characteristics of the postwar world. This interdependence involves risks that were not easy to calculate in advance, but which have been made painfully evident in the wake of the recent oil embargo.

The Arab oil embargo, designed primarily as an instrument to support Arab policy objectives in the Middle East conflict, is interesting from a number of perspectives:

(1) Unlike the conventional perception of economic warfare, where the objective is simply to inflict some substantial losses on a potential opponent in order to limit his war-fighting capability, the Arab embargo was limited to specific diplomatic objectives in a well-defined set of circumstances. The connection between the sought-for behavior of non-Arab states and the termination of the embargo was made explicit by the OPEC nations. As a

---

[2] Quoted in J. R. Schlesinger, *The Political Economy of National Security* (Praeger: New York, 1960), pp. 139-140. An equally renowned economist, John Maynard Keynes, argued that international economic autarky rather than interdependence was preferable because of the tensions which he believed to be inevitable under a system of interdependence. The anti-American nationalism that has been aroused in Canada, South America, and Europe against multinational US firms is a convenient illustration. See J. M. Keynes, "National Self-Sufficiency," *Yale Review* (Summer 1933), pp. 756-758.

result, nations heavily dependent on imported oil (for example, France and Japan) could be induced to cooperate with the OPEC governments conducting the embargo; and this made it more difficult for other countries to organize an effective opposition to it.

(2) The extent to which resource control may be effective as a means of influencing governments does not necessarily imply a total cutoff of deliveries. There can be dramatic political pay-offs from a small cutback, or even a failure to expand production at an anticipated rate. Table 1 shows that the Arab oil embargo involved a reduction of less than ten percent in pre-embargo shipments to the oil importing nations.[3]

(3) Primary or semimanufactured products may be more effective instruments of economic warfare than manufactured products because of higher short-run substitution costs for the former.

Economic warfare may become the gunboat diplomacy of the backward nations of the world. Arab success in influencing the policies of the United States and its allies in the Middle East crisis is subject to at least some degree of emulation by other states or collections of states in certain circumstances.[4]

The question for the United States is whether or not economic warfare can become a useful addition to the range of alternatives available to policymakers in support of diplomatic objectives. The employment of such measures against the Soviet Union to inhibit the transfer of military-related technology has been an important component of US foreign economic policy for 25 years. These efforts

---

[3] A useful review of the Arab oil embargo may be found in R. Johns, "How the Arabs Took Stock of the Power of Their Oil" *Financial Times*, March 22, 1974. Appendix A of the present monograph contains a brief chronology of the Arab oil embargo from its initiation on October 7, 1973, to the lifting of the embargo on March 18, 1974.

[4] The ability of nations exporting raw materials to the industrialized nations of the world is, however, extremely limited at present because of lower costs of substitution for their products in the industrial world, limited ethnic and political cohesion among the nations exporting raw materials, and the limited dependence of most industrial nations on any single raw material. There may be some exceptions, such as titanium, where the supply is dominated by the Soviet Union. The Soviets have demonstrated little reluctance to manipulate resource supplies for political purposes: witness the Soviet cutoff of oil deliveries to the Federal Republic of Germany between October 1973 and January 1974. At the recent UN conference on raw materials policy, some resource-producing nations urged the formation of OPEC-type cartels. This is discussed in more detail in a later section of this essay.

TABLE 1
Arab Oil Shipments, September 1973–January 1974

	September Volume[a]	January Volume[a]	Volume Change	Percent Change
Saudi Arabia	8,569	7,520	−1,049	−12.2
Kuwait	3,526	2,836	−690	−19.6
Abu Dhabi	1,398	1,223	−175	−12.5
Qatar	608	518	−90	−14.8
Oman	302	299	−3	−0.1
Dubai	273	70	+2	+2.9
Libya	2,286	2,032	−254	−11.1
Total Participants	17,030	14,678	−2,352	−13.8
Nonparticipants in Cutbacks				
Iraq	2,112	1,821	−291	−13.8
Iran	5,828	6,137	+309	+5.3
Grand Total	24,970	22,636	−2,334	−9.3

---

[a] In thousands of barrels per day.
Source: *Petroleum Intelligence Weekly.*

have, however, tended to focus on the transfer of industrial technology, because of the perception that such technology was the linchpin of the Soviet (or any modern) military machine. The conviction (with little evidence to support it) was that denial of crucial industrial technology would be the most effective means to inhibit the growth and modernization of the Soviet military establishment.

When the issue is posed in these terms, it tends to obscure the potential impact of more indirect means of waging economic warfare that could be vastly more effective as a way of influencing the character of resource allocation within the Soviet economy, and thereby affecting the resources available to the Soviet defense sector. Moreover, amid the resource abundance we have enjoyed for most of this century, there has been little motivation to consider the utility of economic leverage as an instrument to facilitate access to raw materials or to influence other aspects of our diplomacy.

The most obvious potential instruments of economic warfare available in the structure of US export capabilities are advanced industrial technology and agricultural commodities. Manipulation of the flow of advanced industrial technology as an instrument of economic warfare has several disadvantages. These have become apparent under a variety of circumstances, from wartime restrictions against the Axis powers to peacetime limitations on trade in advanced industrial and scientific technology with the Soviet bloc. To be specific:

(1) The United States does not have a monopoly on advanced industrial and scientific technology. The expertise and production capability for a wide range of advanced technology products exist in most of the West European countries and Japan. Over time, the ability of a target nation to procure advanced technology from nations other than the United States is likely to increase.

(2) There are very few examples of advanced technology that are both essential and unique (that is, for which no substitutes are feasible). In the more typical case, substitutes are available, although at higher cost and reduced efficiency. The effects on either Soviet behavior or capability are likely to be slight. Historically, the Soviets have generally sought to offset their technological inferiority in the military sphere by adding additional manpower (to the detriment of their civilian economy) and by proliferating less sophisticated weapon systems than we have been able to deploy.[5]

(3) It is not easy to measure the contribution of advanced industrial and scientific technology to military effectiveness, because such effectiveness is frequently a byproduct of technology that has

---

[5] For example, the Soviet response to sophisticated manned bomber deployments in the 1950s was not the deployment of equally sophisticated countermeasures such as high performance manned interceptors and surface-to-air missiles (as would have been done by the United States and most West European nations faced with a similar threat). Rather, the Soviets simply proliferated very large numbers of day fighters (primarily the MiG-15 and MiG-17) and SA-1 and SA-2 missiles. This was done at higher cost than would have obtained if sophisticated cost-effective equipment could have been employed. But the Soviet approach did provide an effective air defense system.

broad civilian application. For example, a large-scale scientific computer such as the Control Data CDC-7600 could be effectively employed in many parts of the bureaucratic apparatus of the centrally planned Soviet economy; but it could also be used in the control of radars and missiles in a sophisticated ABM system.[6]

The largest component to our total exports is agriculture. This fact reflects a degree of technological sophistication that borders on monopoly. Since 1968, the value of US agricultural exports has risen from $6 billion to $17 billion or 183 percent, while the value of nonagricultural exports has risen only 79 percent. The employment of agricultural exports as an instrument of economic warfare presents characteristics that are not present in industrial commodities:

(1) The most advanced agricultural technology has been developed and exploited in the United States. As a consequence, there exists a vast capacity for export, especially in raw agricultural commodities (such as wheat, corn, rye, and oats).

(2) The United States is the only nation able to export agricultural commodities in large quantities that has a parallel capacity to augment output in response to changes in worldwide demand. The other major nations with an agricultural export capacity cannot easily increase output, nor do they produce agricultural surpluses in large enough volume substantially to diminish American dominance of the agricultural export market.

(3) The ability of target nations to substitute indigenous production for imports, or to import higher-cost substitutes, is extremely limited. This is especially true in the case of feed grains in the Soviet Union and food grains in the underdeveloped nations.

(4) The US comparative advantage in agriculture is increasing over time relative to that of other nations as a result of a high level of research and investment in agriculture.

---

[6] As, indeed, the US now employs the CDC-7600. It is an integral component of the Site Defense ABM system (for the defense of Minuteman ICBM installations) that is now in research and development.

(5) As per capita income increases in the Soviet Union and other nations, there is a strong desire to enhance the quality of agricultural products consumed. This shift in demand is frequently impossible for the already inadequate agricultural sector to accommodate without massive shifts in domestic resource allocation to the agricultural sector.

(6) Low agricultural productivity in the Soviet Union is difficult to remedy because of an inadequate agricultural infrastructure (such as the absence of adequate interfarm marketing, a rural road net, and so forth) to support increased investment in agricultural technology of the kind commonplace in the United States (such as feedlots for livestock).

The United States has every reason to use this vast agricultural lever in support of its diplomacy. Many of the nations with which it has important conflicts of interest are precisely those whose dependence on US agriculture is likely to be most significant over the near term. The manner in which the conflicts are resolved is important; they may not be capable of politically acceptable resolution through the threat or use of force. The agricultural lever, however, may give US diplomacy improved prospects for success in an international environment where it may be difficult to sustain our foreign policy objectives by other means.

The balance of this essay will examine in detail the potential of agricultural products as an instrument of economic warfare. Chapter Two will review briefly the recent history of economic warfare in the United States. Historically, many policymakers have often expected too much from the employment of such techniques. As a consequence, more realistic opportunities to employ economic warfare in support of foreign policy objectives have frequently been overlooked.

Chapter Three will investigate the capacity of the United States to employ agricultural exports as an instrument of economic warfare. The extent to which a capability can be sustained through 1985 is also discussed in the context of supply-demand projections for agricultural production for that period. Chapter Four will review the character and extent of US (and allied) vulnerability to raw material (except petroleum) supply interruption. Chapter Five will suggest some bureaucratic and institutional mechanisms to facilitate the implementation of this form of economic warfare. Chapter Six will discuss the strategic implications in several alternative circumstances. The Appendix contains a brief chronology of the 1973-74 Arab oil embargo, and several major US policy statements on the subject.

2

US Experience With Economic Warfare

The United States had had economic warfare statutes on the books since 1917. The comprehensiveness and sophistication of these controls have increased sharply since World War II. The first major post-World War II statute, the Export Control Act of 1949, was aimed primarily at the Soviet bloc. This Act, however, gave the President general authority to prohibit or curtail virtually all US exports for any of three purposes: (1) to prevent economic shortages; (2) for national security seasons; and (3) to support US foreign policy objectives.

The broad authority conferred upon the President by this Act has been extended several times, including an amendment in 1962 specifying that export controls should be used to prevent any significant contribution to the military or economic potential of a Communist bloc country through the import of technology from the United States. The Act established a licensing system through the Office of Export Control in the Department of Commerce. The Office of Export Control established a two-tier licensing system. On one level was the general license, which permitted the export of most goods to most countries without specific application by the exporter. The second type, known as a validated license, required specific authorization from appropriate agencies of the US government for exports to Communist bloc countries. The primary criteria for the denial or approval of a validated export license to Communist bloc nations was the degree to which the exported commodities: (1) contributed to the military or economic potential of the country; (2) would be directly applicable for military purposes; and (3) were available in other countries.[7]

In recent years, there has been a gradual relaxation of controls over exports to countries with which trade had hitherto been limited by statute. In 1956, some commodities were exported under general licenses to the Soviet bloc. A year later, Poland was placed in a separate category, for which few products required validated licenses. Rumania was added to this category in 1964. By now, several hundred commodities have been placed on the general license list for exports to East European countries.

In 1969, a new Export Administration Act replaced the Export Control Act of 1949, but maintained the machinery for control of exports. This statute was intended to enhance the prospects for trade having no direct military significance. Its more lenient terms are undergirded, however, by the rigid controls of the Trading with the Enemy Act of 1917, which have been employed to restrict trade with Cuba, North Korea, and North Vietnam. Trade with the Communist bloc countries is further regulated by the Mutual Security Act of 1954, the Agriculture Control Trade and Assistance Act of 1954, and the Mutual Defense Assistance Control Act of 1951 (the "Battle Act"). Through this set of statutory constraints, the 15 NATO nations have established the socalled Coordinating Committee (COCOM) to coordinate NATO restrictions on the flow of militarily significant trade with the Communist bloc countries. There have been some substantial differences in view between the United States and the other COCOM countries, which have regularly been more liberal in their interpretation of the range of goods that should be embargoed. As a result, COCOM countries regularly export commodities to the Soviet bloc which are prohibited to United States exporters.

There is considerable evidence to suggest that statutory measures to support US restrictions on trade with potential or actual enemies

---

[7] A useful discussion of these issues can be found in J. P. Hardt and George D. Holliday, *U.S.-Soviet Commercial Relations, The Interplay of Economics, Technology Transfer, and Diplomacy*, Committee on Foreign Affairs, US House of Representatives, June 10, 1973. This study also discusses related aspects of the transfer of technology by the United States to the Soviet Union.

have been based upon a grossly exaggerated set of expectations. A recent study of the history of US-Soviet trade, and of American efforts to inhibit such trade by statute, argues that economic warfare measures must have a direct major impact on the military or economic potential of an adversary if they are to be successful.[8] US strategy to undermine the military capability of Nazi Germany by saturation bombing of supposed bottlenecks in the German economy was not really successful. While the Germans were prevented from producing adequate supplies of some strategic items, they were nevertheless able to maintain a formidable military capability. "Denials, whether by bombing or embargoes, to be really effective must be very broadly based and nearly complete." Moreover, "at present, in peacetime, even a very tight embargo may be a cause of passing inconvenience and delay, and perhaps a small cost, but no more than that. Small costs like these are especially easy for a centrally-planned economy to bear."[9] Arguing that an embargo must be virtually airtight to achieve a significant effect, the author concludes that a US trade embargo against the Soviet Union could not be very effective in inhibiting Soviet economic and military development.

By thus establishing a very high set of expectations for economic warfare, such techniques have often been dismissed since the mid-1950s, when they were tried and found wanting as almost wholly ineffective. I would argue, however, that this perspective on economic warfare is incorrect, and only serves to discourage US policymakers from taking advantage of one of our most formidable long-term assets, the capacity of the US economy to support our foreign policy objectives. Economic warfare can be effective, and a useful adjunct to other foreign policy initiatives, if only our expectations are put in the proper perpective.[10]

---

[8] F. D. Holzman, "East-West Trade and Investment Policy Issues: Past and Future", in *Soviet Economic Prospects for the 70's*, Joint Economic Committee, US Congress, June 27, 1973.
[9] *Ibid.*, p. 663.
[10] After considerable experience with interdiction bombing, the US Air Force has learned that what could be expected from this strategy were important dislocations, slowdowns in deliveries to battlefield destinations, reduction in the number of days an opponent could engage in firefights, and general confusion in enemy logistics. When these revised expectations are embodied in the planning process, an interdiction campaign can be extremely successful. The combination of an effective ground campaign by UN forces in Korea, maintaining pressure on the Chinese Communists to expend their munitions inventory, and aeriel bombardment to reduce the flow of materiel to the front, resulted in the defeat of the Chinese forces while inflicting over one million casualties on them.

Economic warfare cannot be expected to carry the entire burden of containing a strong and aggressive power. As one of several coordinated elements in a broad foreign policy strategy, however, economic warfare can make an important contribution to achieving long-term foreign policy objectives in relation to the Soviet Union and other nations, and can be highly effective in the short term. Economic warfare can be a useful device for affecting the pattern of resource allocation within the target country. Denial of trade in some areas, while encouraging it in others, can alter the pattern of growth in an economy that favors one sector while leaving another dependent upon foreign resources.[11]

With regard to the Soviet Union, one of our most potent assets is our consistent ability to supply agricultural exports to meet shortfalls in Soviet domestic production. The Soviets have made a major policy decision to alter the main source of protein from food grains to livestock. The 1971-75 economic plan sets rather ambitious goals for increasing the production of basic agricultural commodities some 3.5 percent above the 1970 level. The plan also calls for a ten percent increase in investment in fixed assets, new construction, and machinery and equipment. When one allows for the impact of favorable weather upon the base year, 1970, the required annual increase will have to be a third higher, or 4.5 perceent, to meet the objectives set.[12]

The overall increase in inputs to the agricultural sector—primarily industry inputs—will undoubtedly strain Soviet industrial capacity. This is likely to be especially true for construction materials and agricultural fertilizers. The broad details of the plan are summarized below.[13]

> Investment directly into agriculture is scheduled to be nearly 129 billion rubles (about $172 billion) during 1971-75.[14] Meeting this goal will require agricultural investments to grow an

[11] There is recent evidence that the economic warfare conducted by the Arab League—the practice of the Arab Boycott Office of prohibiting foreign firms from transacting business with member nations if they do certain types of business in Israel—has had some success. The boycott has successfully prevented the Israelis from broadening their industrial base. Despite numerous devaluations, the Israeli balance of payments (merchandise) has never been in surplus. See Alain Cass, "Assessing the Effects of the Boycott," *Financial Times*, November 21, 1974.

[12] D. B. Diamond and C. B. Kruger, "Recent Developments in Output and Productivity in Soviet Agriculture," in *Soviet Economic Prospects for the 70's*, p. 319.

[13] *Ibid.*, p. 320.

[14] The nominal value of the ruble is 0.75 rubles to US $1. Conversion at this value gives a rough idea of the magnitude of economic quantities involved in the program.

average of 9.5 percent a year and to rise as a share of all invest-ments from 23.5 precent in 1970 to 27.5 percent in 1975.

Total investment in machinery and equipment (producer dur-ables) for farms during 1971-75 is planned to be 35.5 billion rubles, a 54 percent increase over the value of such deliveries to farms in the last half of the 1960s.

About one fifth of total investment in agriculture is to be ex-pended on land amelioration, mostly reclamation by irrigation and drainage. The boost in investment in land reclamation is to result in an expansion of about 30 percent in the stock of irri-gated and drained land. In support of the reclamation effort, Soviet industry is to deliver new construction equipment into agriculture in an amount equal to nearly 90 percent of the total inventory of such equipment in the overall construction sector at the end of 1970.

In addition to a step-up in the flow of investment goods to agriculture, the flows of other types of industrially produced goods to farms are to be expanded. Overall deliveries of major types of producer goods used in current productive activity in agriculture are to rise at an average annual rate of 6.5 percent during 1971-75.[15] Especially noteworthy are a scheduled rise of two thirds in the use of fertilizer and a significant growth in use of plant protection materials (pesticides and herbicides). The required increase in production of these goods will necessitate further large investments in the chemical industry.

All of the 19.5 percent increase in output for the period 1971-75 is to come from the country's collective and state farms. Production from individual holdings, which contributed 30 per-cent of total output in 1970, is implicitly slated to decline slowly in the 1971-75 period.

As a result, if the initial plans for output in the private sector are carried out, the above measures for achieving a rapid ad-vance in output in the socialized sector may be partially offset.

---

[15] The major types of producer goods included here are fertilizer, electric power, fuels and lubricants, current repair services, rubber products, industrially produced feeds, and lime.

This major increase in agricultural investment is especially important from the perspective of international trade in agricultural commodities. There is likely to be a sustained Soviet requirement for the importation of food and feed grains if the livestock production goals are to be retained. As a consequence, it is expected that the Soviet Union will be a major importer of grain for the next three to five years, and perhaps beyond, as a consequence of the great variability of yields of Soviet agriculture. The only major grain exporting areas of the world are North America and Australia. Of these areas, only the United States has the capability of being an exporter on the scale required by the Soviet Union. In these circumstances, what might be accomplished by using agricultural exports as an instrument of economic warfare?

It is not reasonable to expect that denial of United States agricultural exports to the Soviet Union would bring the Soviet economy to its knees. In fact, with a few rare exceptions, virtually every modern economy is immune from crippling economic warfare of this variety. What economic warfare *can* do in these circumstances is the following:

(1) Because imports of grains are important to the Soviet plan for agriculture, denial of these grains can have an important impact on agricultural resource allocation within the Soviet Union, and consequently affect the success of the plan.

(2) In order to make the agricultural plan effective, in the absence of United States grain imports, the Soviets would be forced to take resources away from other sectors of the economy, especially the defense sector.

(3) The Soviet agricultural plan is politically important, not only for reasons of economic autarky, but also to restructure the system of incentives in order to raise productivity in other sectors of the economy. Thus, it will not be lightly abandoned.

(4) The political stake that the Soviets have in the success of their agricultural program may open up diplomatic opportunities for the United States to obtain a political *quid pro quo* for our agricultural exports.

Similar opportunities in other circumstances will be discussed at a later stage. These opportunities arise chiefly from the US position as a major food exporter to regions of the world whose agriculture is inadequate to support domestic needs. If one's expectations as to the effectiveness of manipulating foreign agricultural sales are distorted by the World War II notion of bringing an opponent to heel, then economic warfare is likely to be a failure. On the other hand, if one views economic warfare as a device for significantly influencing the behavior of potential adversaries, then such a strategy can make a useful contribution to the achievement of foreign policy objectives without resort to the threat or use of force.

Economic Warfare in Chile

The economic history of the inept government[16] of Salvadore Allende in Chile during the years 1970 to 1973 provides an interesting example of the linkage between economic viability and political stability. The events in Chile cannot be characterized as economic warfare within the normal definition of the term. Unquestionably, there was economic conflict between the United States and Chile, primarily stemming from Chile's nationalization—without compensation—of the US-owned copper industry and the reciprocal reluctance of US government agencies to extend substantial credits to the regime.[17]

Chile declared a moratorium in November 1971 on the payment of foreign debts. This step was taken in order to make foreign exchange available to finance the Allende regime's various land reform and redistribution schemes. As a consequence, US and other foreign firms became unwilling to extend credit to finance Chilean purchases of spare parts for industry. This had some effect on Chilean industrial production, although Communist ideology also intervened so extensively in the operation and management of Chilean industry that in many cases, production was halted entirely. Overall industrial pro-

---

[16] In the words of the Socialist economist, Paul N. Rosenstein-Rodan, Salvatore Allende fell "not because he was a Socialist, but because he was incompetent." See "Why Allende Failed," *Challenge*, May-June 1974.

[17] President Nixon issued a formal statement in January 1972 to the effect that the United States would not extend new bilateral economic assistance, and would oppose multilateral loans, to nations expropriating US interests without taking "reasonable steps" toward compensation. Quoted in P. E. Sigmund, "The 'Invisible Blockade' and the Overthrow of Allende," *Foreign Affairs*, January 1974.

duction declined rapidly. The result was to inflict stark losses on the Chilean middle class, contributing to their restiveness and politicization and ultimately facilitating the overthrow of the Allende regime.

As US and multilateral lending institutions were reducing their lending operations, the shortfall was more than offset by Soviet bloc efforts to prop up the tottering Allende regime. Between 1971 and 1973, the lending of US and multilateral lending institutions declined $361.6 million over the pre-Allende period, while aid from Soviet and other Socialist sources (excluding Communist China) totaled $620 million. The tables below display the distribution of aid sources during the Allende period.

The significance of the Allende experience is that developing economies may be extraordinarily vulnerable to relatively small increments of economic instability. In Chile, where copper production accounts

US and Multilateral Aid Authorizations to Chile,
1968–70 and 1971–73
(In millions of US dollars)

US aid	1968–70	1971–73[a]	Difference
AID	111.3	3.3	108.0
Peace Corps	4.3	1.7	2.6
Public Law 480	45.2	14.7	30.5
Eximbank[b]	128.8	21.6	107.2
Subtotal	289.6	41.3	248.3
Multilateral aid:			
IBRD	30.9	0	30.9
IDB	94.0	11.6[c]	82.4
Subtotal	124.9	11.6	113.3
Total	414.5	52.9	361.6

[a] In general, up to September 11, 1973.
[b] Includes credit guarantees and insurance.
[c] Two credits totaling $11,600,000 were authorized by the IDB for two Chilean universities (Universidad Catolica and Universidad Austral).
Source: Official statistics from the individual institutions.

Foreign Credits Authorized For Chile From Government
and International Agency Sources
1971–73
(In millions of US dollars)

	1971–73
I. United States	$41.3
AID	3.3
Public Law 480	14.7
Peace Corps	1.7
Eximbank	21.6[a]
II. USSR	260.5[b]
III. Other Socialist countries	359.5
China	(97.0)
IV. Latin American countries	134.0
V. Western Europe and Japan	142.0
VI. International lending agencies	11.6
IDB	(11.6)
Total	947.9

[a] Includes credit insurance and guarantees.
[b] Includes short-term ($98,500,000) and long-term ($162,000,000) credits.

Sources: I: US official sources; II: CORFO, Republic of Chile; III: CORFO, Republic of Chile; IV: Foreign Ministry, Republic of Chile; V: Foreign Ministry, Republic of Chile; VI: Inter-American Development Bank.

for most of foreign exchange earnings, 95 percent of the spare parts to maintain mining equipment originated in the United States. This suggests that had economic warfare been systematically conducted by the United States (as opposed to the haphazard manner in which the Allende regime blundered into a situation where a lack of international confidence was assured), the regime might have collapsed in 1972 or early 1973.

The Arab Oil Embargo

By the most routine measures of success, the Arab oil embargo against the United States and the curtailment of supplies to the nations of Western Europe and Japan was an effective exercise of economic warfare. A cost was imposed upon the target nations compelling a substantial reallocation of resources that would not have been made in the absence of the embargo. Moreover, the United States is now embarked upon a $1 trillion, ten-year program to minimize its dependence on foreign energy sources; an effort that would not have been launched in the absence of OPEC-sponsored economic warfare. The OPEC countries also acquired a new stature in international politics, and the diplomacy of Western Europe, Japan, and to some degree the United States has shifted significantly, if not decisively, against Israel.

This change in the international environment occurred as a consequence of less than a ten-percent reduction in petroleum output over a four-month period. The Arab oil-producing states (OAPEC) had to reduce their output by 30 percent in order to effect a four percent reduction in total US energy consumption during the October 1973 —January 1974 period; and despite considerable "leaking" and swapping in the market, the limited economic success had visible political benefits.

The effectiveness of the embargo against the United States coincided with rapidly rising US imports of petroleum. A previous effort by Saudi Arabia during the 1956 Arab-Israeli War to cut back oil deliveries failed because the Western countries were not yet vulnerable to such action. From virtually zero imports in 1970, the United States imported nearly ten percent of its petroleum requirements from OAPEC sources three years later. This explosion in US imports created the vulnerability which made the United States susceptible to economic warfare. The problem is exacerbated by the high average price of Persian Gulf oil—over $10 per barrel (compared to the marginal cost of production of ten to 50 cents per barrel). This price is substantially above the revenue-maximizing price of $7 to $8 per barrel, suggesting a price motivated by economic warfare considerations rather than the traditional economic motives of a cartel.[18]

---

[18] The Western nations appear to be ready to link this current high price to an index. If the price of oil were linked to a commodity index in the year OPEC was formed (1960), the current oil price should only be $3.40; if it were linked to the prices of industrial exports, the price of oil would be only $2.50 today. Even if it were linked to the free market price of gold, the price of oil would be $6.40 today. This proposal is a good example of how to make a bad situation worse. "Index Linked Oil Oozes Closer" *Economist*, January 4-10, 1975, p. 67.

What stands out most conspicuously from the US experience with the oil embargo is (1) the amount of "leverage" over US diplomacy associated with a small marginal change in petroleum deliveries, and (2) the limited discussion thus far of US policy alternatives falling between acquiescence and military intervention and the occupation of the Persian Gulf.

3

Agricultural Exports as an Instrument of Economic Warfare

US Export Supply

The United States, in particular, and North America in general, are the principal sources of agricultural commodities for the world market. The US lead in agriculture is greater than Arab dominance of the petroleum market. This dominance has been growing as a consequence of a multiplicity of factors, such as declining agricultural productivity in some regions (and especially in the Soviet Union), a high birth rate, the shift in climatological patterns in North Africa, and the shift in taste from low quality protein (direct consumption of grain) to high quality protein (livestock) as a consequence of rising per capita income. Table 2 indicates world production trends since the early 1960s.

While world agricultural production has increased 30 percent since 1960, per capita production has increased only two percent in the developing nations. This is the result of population increases outstripping the 29 percent increase in aggregate agricultural production in these nations. The developed nations of the world increased in production by a similar magnitude (31 percent), but were able to increase per capita consumption by 17 percent because of more moderate population growth. Those data conceal great differences among the

TABLE 2
World Agricultural Production, 1966-73

Total Agricultural Production
(1961-65 = 100)

Year	World[a]	Developed Countries[b]	Developing Countries[c]
1961-65	100	100	100
1966	108	110	105
1967	112	113	110
1968	116	117	114
1969	117	116	119
1970	120	118	123
1971	124	123	126
1972	123	123	124
1973	130	131	129

Per Capita Agricultural Production
(1961-65 = 100)

Year	World[a]	Developed Countries[b]	Developing Countries[c]
1961-65	100	100	100
1966	102	106	97
1967	104	108	100
1968	105	111	101
1969	104	109	102
1970	105	110	103
1971	107	113	103
1972	104	112	99
1973	108	117	102

[a] Excludes Communist Asia.
[b] North America, Europe, USSR, Japan, Republic of South Africa, Australia, and New Zealand.
[c] Latin America, Asia (except Japan and Communist Asia), Africa (except Republic of South Africa).
Source: Overseas Development Council.

nations of the world. Many have actually experienced substantial retrogression in recent years.[19]

Because of dwindling world grain reserves, the ability of the world agricultural economy to respond to shortfalls in supply is increasingly dependent upon North American, and principally US, agricultural exports. Table 3 summarizes recent grain reserve trends on a world-wide basis.

TABLE 3

World Grain Reserves, 1961-74

Year	Reserve Stocks of Grain	Grain Equivalent of Idled US Cropland	Total Reserves	Reserves as Share of Annual Grain Consumption	
	(millions of metric tons)			(percent)	(no. of days)
1961	154	68	222	26	95
1962	131	81	212	24	88
1963	125	70	195	21	77
1964	128	70	198	21	77
1965	113	71	184	19	69
1966	99	79	178	18	66
1967	100	51	151	15	55
1968	116	61	177	17	62
1969	136	73	209	19	69
1970	146	71	217	19	69
1971	120	41	161	14	51
1972	131	78	209	18	66
1973	105	20	125	10	37
1974[a]	89	0	89	7	27

[a] Projection.
Source: Overseas Development Council.

[19] A UPI dispatch (April 8, 1974) reports that India's grain production has fallen seven million metric tons short of the government's target, indicating that India would be in the market for substantial quantities. India's disastrous drought-induced food crisis of 1966-67 required the importation of ten million tons of grain. World grain reserves, however, have been reduced from 178 million metric tons (equivalent to 66 days of consumption) to an estimated 89 million metric tons (27 days) in 1974. The consequences of a major crop failure in India this year could be grave.

Historically, increases in agricultural output have come as a consequence of increases in planted acreage and yields per acre. (Table 3 indicates that the former option is no longer available in the United States; cropland acreage withheld from planting has declined from 60 million acres in 1972 to zero in 1974.) There have also been substantial improvements in the yield per acre in cereal production as a result of improved technology—particularly in high-yield strains of wheat and rice. In some cases, particularly Pakistan, the yield per acre has nearly doubled.[20]

As noted earlier, however, as per capita income increases there is a marked change in preference in favor of the consumption of high quality protein, especially livestock. In these circumstances, livestock convert high protein feed grains into beef, pork, and poultry. On a per capita basis, the average American consumes over one ton of grain per year, only 150 pounds of which are consumed directly; the remainder is consumed indirectly in the form of animal protein.[21] It is in the production of feed grains that the United States has its most conspicuous and enduring predominance.

The United States, which exports 75 percent of total North American feed grains in the international market, is also dominant in soybean production, the most important source of livestock protein. Throughout the 1960s and 1970s, the United States produced 90 percent of the world's exports of soybeans.[22] Moreover, because of the importance of soybeans to the diet of both the developed world (in the form of indirect consumption through livestock) and the underdeveloped world (nearly one billion people consume soybean products directly as a protein source), that dominance is likely to continue for many years to come. With the exception of Brazil, which has begun to produce soybeans, the United States is the only nation with a significant surplus available to the international export market. The ability of the United States to expand soybean production is limited, however, by technology and the absence of unplanted acreage. In recent years, the major portion of the fourfold increase in the

---

[20] L. R. Brown, *World Without Borders* (Vintage: New York, 1973), p. 98. These developments are popularly known as the Green Revolution.
[21] *Ibid.*, p. 96.
[22] *Ibid.*, p. 98. The value of soybean exports exceeds the dollar value of computers, jet aircraft, and wheat.

soybean crop (85 percent) has come about as a consequence of additional planting of soybeans. Increases in yields are not vulnerable to the technological changes we have experienced with wheat and rice.[23]

While there has been a fourfold increase in the production of soybeans since 150, yields per acre have increased only one percent (one fourth of the average annual increase for corn over the same period). Nongrain substitutes for protein are difficult to obtain. The most important, fish, has been a declining source of protein since 1969, after increasing at a five percent annual rate since 1950. Moreover, several of the 30 kinds of commercial grade fish now taken will not sustain the current level of catch.[24] Advanced technological efforts to produce synthetic forms of protein from petroleum are not yet a cost-effective solution, and may not be so for several years. This situation has led one observer to note:[25]

> We may be witnessing the transformation of the world protein market from a buyer's market to a seller's market, much as the world energy market has been transformed over the past few years.

The Worldwide Demand for Agricultural Imports

As a consequence of several factors, including organizational shortcomings, inadequate investment in agriculture, increasing population, climatological shifts, and increasing per capita income, there has been a worldwide increase in the demand for agricultural products from the surplus-producing nations of the world. Since 1971, US food grain exports have nearly doubled, from 16.9 million metric tons to 31 million metric tons in 1973-74 (estimated). Moreover, worldwide exports from the major producing nations have increased by 27 percent over the same period. The export of food grains reflects substantial shortfalls in many parts of the underdeveloped world as a result of extended droughts.

---

[23] The soybean is a legume with a built-in supply of nitrogen, and consequently is not susceptible to nitrogen fertilizer. *Ibid.*, p. 14.
[24] *Ibid.*, p. 15.
[25] *Ibid.*, p. 17.

TABLE 5
Feed Grains: Production, Exports, and Imports
Selected Countries and Regions[28]
(in millions of metric tons)

	1971-72	1972-73	1973-74 (est.)
Exports			
Canada	4.4	3.6	3.5
Australia	3.2	1.8	1.9
Argentina	6.3	4.3	7.1
South Africa	2.2	3.3	0.3
Thailand	2.3	1.4	2.3
Western Europe	11.4	11.0	11.5
USA	20.7	35.5	37.3
World Total	53.4.	62.6	66.0
Imports			
Western Europe	26.4	28.0	29.0
Japan	10.0	21.0	13.1
USSR	3.9	4.9	5.0
Eastern Europe	5.0	3.7	3.7
World Total	53.4	62.6	66.0
Production			
Canada	22.2	18.9	19.2
Australia	5.8	3.6	5.3
Argentina	9.5	15.5	15.6
South Africa	10.2	4.6	10.0
Thailand	2.3	1.4	2.6
USSR	70.6	70.2	85.0
Eastern Europe	50.1	55.1	55.3
USA	189.7	181.9	191.9
World Total	563.4	544.8	578.4
Consumption			
World Total	547.7	563.4	582.4

---

[28] *Ibid.*

TABLE 6
Net Soviet Grain Trade
1955-56—1972-73

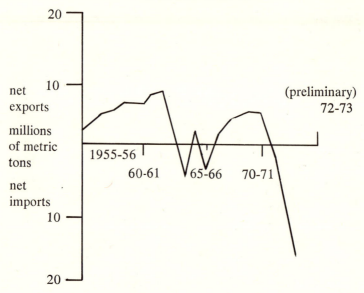

Source: Brown, "The Next Crisis, Food?" *loc. cit.*, p. 8.

ularly feed grains, will be necessary. A recent study of the Soviet agricultural sector published by the Joint Economic Committee of the Congress emphasized these points:[29]

> Soviet prospects for catching up with US farm output by 1975 are poor. The continuation in 1971 of a sharp fall in Soviet crops and a record harvest in the US put the gap in crop production below the 1966 level. An even worse harvest in 1972 eroded the Soviet position further. Although Soviet leaders are counting on substantial gains in 1973-75 to bring production back in line with the original 1971-75 plan goals, the actual gains are very unlikely to bring the USSR's farm output up to 1970 US output by 1975.

[29] F. D. Whitehouse and J. F. Havelka, "Comparison of Farm Output in the US and USSR, 1950-1971," in *Soviet Economic Prospects for the 70's*, p. 356-358.

The 1971-75 plan goals for the production of meat, eggs, and cotton could be achieved, but the increase in targets for production of milk, grain, sugar beets, and sunflower seeds, are probably beyond reach (see Table 7). In order to produce an average of 195 million (gross) tons of grain in 1971-75, for example, the USSR would have to get an average crop of 211 million tons in 1973-75—43 million tons more than 1972 crop. Even if achieved, this would not yield enough net usable grain to come up to the US level of 1970.

More important, the USSR surely will face increasing difficulties in 1973-75 in meeting requirements for grain from domestic resources if the leadership holds to its commitment to strengthen the livestock sector. As indicated above, the expansion of livestock herds and increased feed rations per animal, coupled with

TABLE 7

USSR: Progress in Meeting 1971-75 Plan Goals
for Agriculture[a]
(in millions of metric tons)

	Goals for average production in 1971-75	Average actual production in 1971-72[b]	Average production needed in 1973-75 to meet 1971-75 goals
Grain	195.0	171.0	211.0
Potatoes	[c]	85.1	[c]
Vegetables	[c]	20.0	[c]
Cotton	7.0–7.2	7.2	6.9–7.2
Sugar beets	87.5	73.9	96.6
Sunflower seeds	6.7	5.5	7.5
Meat	14.3	13.5	14.8
Milk	92.3	83.2	98.4
Eggs[d]	46.7	46.7	46.7
Wood	.464	.422	.492

[a] Official production data are presented in this table to permit a comparison of actual production with plan goals. In the case of grain and sunflower seeds, the gross production overstates significantly the net usable output—by an average of about eight percent for sunflower seeds and 19 percent for grain.
[b] Based on preliminary estimates of 1972 production and actual production in 1971.
[c] Not available.
[d] Billions of eggs.

continued inefficiency in converting feed to live weight, have raised Soviet requirements for feed substantially. At the same time, yields of forage crops have virtually stagnated, placing the burden of supporting the livestock program on feed grains. The USSR, however, will not be able to grow the corn and soybeans which are the basis of US rations. Thus, Brezhnev's livestock program, it is maintained, will become increasingly costly, in part because of a continuing need to buy foreign grain.

Many other factors will influence farm production in both the US and USSR—political developments as well as economic constraints. Unusual developments in export demand, for example, could result in more rapid growth of US output, using land now held out of production to meet output needs. In the USSR, on the other hand, the further expansion of farm output depends largely on resources and technology still untested under Soviet conditions and on policies not fully formulated. Continued Soviet purchases of US feed grains no doubt will stimulate both USSR output of livestock products and US output of feed grains. The uncertainty surrounding future grain purchases notwithstanding, an extension of recent trends in US and USSR farm outputs suggests that Soviet production might increase to only about 85-88 percent of US output by 1975.

For different reasons, circumstances in the underdeveloped world also suggest a continued interest in purchasing US agricultural imports. Historically, the nations of Africa and Asia were self-sufficient in grain production; but this has changed since the mid-1930s. They have gone from a net exporting position of three million metric tons exported annually in the 1934-38 period, to a net importing position of 43 million metric tons in 1973, according to an Overseas Development Council estimate.[30]

Table 8 points out the dramatic shifts that have taken place in the past four decades in the distribution of net grain importers and exporters. The most conspicuous aspect of this shifting pattern is the

---

[30] During a severe drought in India in 1966, one third of the 34 million tons imported by Asian nations was imported by India. Droughts could vastly increase import demands on a periodic basis.

TABLE 8
The Changing Pattern of World Grain[a]

	1934-38	1948-52	1960	1966	1973[b]
		(millions of metric tons)			
North America	+5	+23	+39	+59	+88
Latin America	+9	+1	0	+5	—4
Western Europe	—24	—22	—25	—27	—21
Eastern Europe and USSR	+5	—	0	—4	—27
Africa	+1	0	—2	—7	—4
Asia	+2	—6	—17	—34	—39
Australia and New Zealand	+3	+3	+6	+8	+7

[a] Plus sign denotes net exports; minus sign denotes net imports.
[b] Estimate.
Source: Overseas Development Council.

almost total dependence of much of the world on North American grain production.

This dependence is more stark than the dependence of Western Europe and Japan on Middle Eastern oil, primarily because of the inadequate character and high costs of substitutes for US agricultural products as compared to the intermediate and long-term substitution possibilities for petroleum.

These increases in demand, when set against supply shortfalls and changes in taste in the developed world, have left a very formidable burden on the underdeveloped nations. Since FY 1972, the grain imports of the underdeveloped nations of the world have increased from 20.6 million metric tons to 26.7 million in FY 1974.[31] At the same time, there has been a 207 percent increase in the price of grain, and this more seriously inhibits the development of many of the nations involved than the increase in the price of petroleum in recent years.

---

[31] US Department of Agriculture estimate.

As a consequence of unfolding events affecting both the supply and demand for agricultural commodities on a worldwide basis, the United States has—without planning for it—acquired an unparalleled capacity for influencing international economic welfare through manipulation of agricultural exports. Stated simply, the combination of an increasing worldwide demand for the agricultural products the United States produces in abundance, and the absence of significant alternative sources of production, will place the United States in a unique peacetime position. We have, in short, an effective near-monopoly of the raw materials of subsistence. For the near and inter-mediate term, moreover, the inevitable growth of foreign demand and the dominating position of US supply make it likely that this situation will continue for several years.

The strategic implications of these unforeseen circumstances have not been widely explored, nor have the tactics for exploiting them been developed in a systematic manner. The following chapters of this essay will attempt to sketch some of the strategic dimensions of the situation, as well as how they might be exploited to advance the national inter-ests of the United States.

US Agricultural Exports Through 1985

The dominance of the United States in the international market for agricultural products appears to be a significant medium- to long-term political and economic strength. This is because a substantial fraction of the world's population lives in areas where the demand for agri-cultural products exceeds the likely indigenous supply for the next decade (through 1985).

The figures in Table 9 below emphasize the enormous disparity be-tween the developed and the developing nations of the world in terms of the growth of food and feed grain requirements between 1970 and 1985. In feed grain requirements, for example, indigenous produc-tion must more than double between 1970 and 1985 simply to meet demand. Thus, the developing nations must expand food production by 67 percent over the entire 1970-85 period, while developed (non-Communist) countries need only expand output by approximately

26 percent to meet demand. On average, production in the developed nations is likely to exceed this figure (26 percent), while the under-developed nations will probably experience a substantial shortfall. The Communist economies of the Soviet Union and Eastern Europe should be capable meeting basic food requirements through 1985. But because of traditional problems of storage loss and an inadequate transportation and distribution system, combined with the Soviet shift to livestock as a protein source, they will continue to be net importers through the mid-1980s.

Similarly, in high protein-content food products, the developing nations tend to have a demand growth rate that is 50 percent higher

TABLE 9
Projections of Food Demand vs.
Food Production to 1985

Area	Volume Indices		Volume Growth Rates	
	De-mand	Pro-duction	De-mand	Pro-duction
	1969-71 = 100		Percent Per Annum	
Developed countries	127	151	1.6	2.8
Market economies	126	143	1.5	2.4
Eastern Europe and USSR	132	168	1.8	3.5
Developing market economies	172	146	3.7	2.6
Africa	177	145	3.9	2.5
Asia and Far East	167	143	3.5	2.4
Latin America	171	152	3.6	2.9
Near East	186	157	4.2	3.1
Asian centrally-planned economies	159	146	3.1	2.6
All developing countries	167	146	3.5	2.6
World	145	150	2.5	2.7

Source: *Present Food Situation and Dimensions and Causes of Hunger and Malnutrition in the World*, Preparatory Committee of the World Food Conference, ECOSOC, May 1974.

than the world average, and frequently twice that of the developed
nations of the world. The figures cited in Table 10 for selected protein-
source products illustrate the disparity between the demand growth
rate of developing nations and that of the world as a whole to meet
the 1985 demand for high protein products, including meat, fish,
cereals, and starchy roots.

TABLE 10
Selected Foods—A Comparison of Demand Growth
1970-85

	World	Developing Countries
Demand for fish	3.4 percent per year	4.8 percent per year
Demand for meat	3.1 percent per year	4.7 percent per year
Demand for cereals	2.1 percent per year	3.9 percent per year
Demand for starchy roots	1.4 percent per year	2.6 percent per year

The disparity between the developed and developing nations in
terms of requirements to meet demand through 1985 is most starkly
reflected in the projections given in Table 11. While the total cereal
requirements for the world will increase 39 percent by 1985 over 1970
consumption, developing nations must increase their feed grain production by 107 percent over this period, while the developed nations
of the world need only increase their production approximately one
third of that amount, or 36 percent. Similarly, to meet anticipated
1985 food grain requirements, the developed nations of the world
need only increase their output by three percent by 1985, while the
developing nations must increase their output 16 times that amount,
or 48 percent, to meet anticipated demands.

As a consequence, the long-term demand for imported raw agricultural commodities by the developing nations of the world and the
Soviet Union is likely to remain strong through 1985. The level of
demand can be influenced by the extent to which belt-tightening
measures are politically acceptable in the nations involved. Alternatively, the situation in major deficit nations such as India and the
Soviet Union could be changed dramatically through major institutional changes. Both India and the Soviet Union have vast acreages

TABLE 11
Additional Agricultural Output Required
to Satisfy Increase in World Demand

		Percentage increase 1970 vs. 1985
Total cereal requirements (Food, feed, and nonfood)	+ 470 million tons	39
Feed grain requirements[a]	+ 180 million tons	43
Developed countries	+ 133 million tons	36
Developing countries	+ 49 million tons	107
Food grain requirements	+ 236 million tons	37
Developed countries	+ 5 million tons	3
Developing countries	+ 231 million tons	48

[a] Assuming no substantial changes in production techniques, but continuing modest improvements in feed conversion efficiency.

under cultivation; but the manner in which agricultural production is organized makes it impossible for these nations to meet their objectives with indigenous production. Changes in the direction of market-oriented agriculture in these two countries could bring about an abrupt change in their dependence on agricultural imports. The persistence of their preference for the existing mode of agriculture, however, suggests that such change is unlikely to emerge over the next decade. As a consequence, their deficit status is likely to endure. The agricultural problems of the smaller nations of the developing world are more intractable, and can only be reversed by massive amounts of capital investment to modernize agriculture—an event that appears at least as unlikely as major organizational change in Soviet and Indian agriculture.

The Outlook for the United States as a Supplier of Agricultural Exports, 1975-85

The United States has been the preeminent supplier of raw agricultural commodities to the international market for most of this century as a consequence of the scale of its agricultural production and the higher level of technology. Improvements in technology are directly expressed in yield per acre of a particular raw agricultural commodity. For the most part, improvements in yield have arisen as a consequence of improved fertilizer technology, irrigation, and rationalized production, harvesting, and storage techniques. Since the appearance of major worldwide shortages in key raw agricultural commodities in the early 1970s, substantial additions to output have occurred as a consequence of increased acreage devoted to agriculture. The increased level of plantings has been induced by the general upward movement of prices for raw agricultural commodities as the supply situation tightened in many parts of the world, particularly the Soviet Union, India, and Africa. The United States possesses a total cropland inventory of approximately 736 million acres. As of 1970, 330 million acres were employed directly as cropland, while 51 million acres were held for soil improvement and not used for planting, and 88 million acres were retained as cropland pasture. A potential inventory of an additional 264 million acres could be shifted to agricultural use. But only a small portion of the available acreage is likely to be shifted to cropland use because of competition between forestry and agriculture, and also because of continuing high livestock prices, which tend to slow the shift from pasture and range to cropland.

The amount of acreage required to supply domestic markets should decline from the 1970 figure to 292 million acres by 1980. This decline reflects technological improvements, resulting in improved yields per acre, an abundance of water available for agricultural uses, and declining US birthrates. This development implies that the amount of acreage available for production of raw agricultural products for the international market will increase.[32] Approximately 350 million acres of harvested cropland will be available for agricultural use by 1985. and over 20 percent of that land will be available to support agricultural production for export.

By 1985, substantial increases in output of raw agricultural commodities are likely as a consequence of higher levels of planting and improved agricultural technology. The data presented in Table 12 suggest the extent to which output of agricultural products is likely to increase. We may anticipate an 88 percent increase in corn output

---

[32] Despite journalistic impressions to the contrary, highways and airports account for only one percent of the total land area.

TABLE 12
US Agricultural Production Capabilities (1969-85)
Past, Current, and Projected Yields
(Average)

Yields		Acreage		Output	Average Annual Percentage Growth of Output 1969-85
Corn				*Billions of*	
Bushels per Acre		*Million Acres*		*Bushels*	
1969-71	82.2	1969-71	58.7	4.83	
1972	96.9	1972	57.3	5.55	
1973	92.4	1973	61.5	5.68	5.84 percent
1980	109.5	1980	73.7	8.07	
1985	120.0	1985	75.5	9.06	
Soybeans				*Billions of*	
Bushels per Acre		*Million Acres*		*Bushels*	
1969-71	27.4	1969-71	42.1	1.15	
1972	28.0	1972	45.8	1.28	
1973	28.0	1973	56.2	1.57	6.49 percent
1980	32.0	1980	64.1	2.05	
1985	34.5	1985	65.7	2.27	
Feed Grains				*Millions*	
Tons per Acre		*Million Acres*		*of Tons*	
1969-71	1.81	1969-71	100.4	181.72	
1972	2.13	1972	94.1	200.43	
1973	2.03	1973	102.4	207.87	4.88 percent
1980	2.47	1980	114.7	283.31	
1985	2.72	1985	115.7	314.70	
Wheat				*Billions of*	
Bushels per Acre		*Million Acres*		*Bushels*	
1969-71	31.9	1969-71	46.1	1.47	
1972	32.7	1972	47.3	1.55	
1973	31.8	1973	53.7	1.71	3.67 percent
1980	34.5	1980	62.3	2.15	
1985	36.6	1985	62.3	2.28	

Source: *American Agriculture—Its Capacity to Produce,* US Department of Agriculture, Washington, February 1974.

and a 97 percent increase in soybean output by 1985 over the 1969-71 average. Feed grains and wheat are expected to be 73 and 55 percent higher, respectively, than they were in the 1969-71 base period.

The most impressive improvements in technology will occur in corn and feed grain production, where increases in yield per acre are anticipated to increase 46 percent for corn and 50 percent for feed grains. As a consequence of the improved yields for corn and feed grains, acreage is not expected to increase as rapidly. Only a 29 percent increase in acreage is required to increase corn production 88 percent, and only a 15 percent increase in feed grain acreage is necessary for a 73 percent increase in feed grain production.

The robust health of US agriculture can be an important source of strength, because it virtually assures that we will not be vulnerable to nonindigenous supply interruptions over the next decade. The nature of human requirements for agricultural products makes this a very useful element in support of foreign policy. Moreover, if the relatively high rate of US investment in agriculture is sustained, the current US advantage in agricultural technology is likely to be enhanced. This is because most of the long-range solutions to a worldwide food shortage tend to be capital-intensive. These techniques include hydroponics, trickle culture, aquaculture, growth chambers, single-cell proteins, selective breeding techniques, desert reclamation, and others.

4

US Vulnerability To Raw Material Supply Interruption

The ability of the oil exporting nations to improve their terms of trade as opposed to the consuming nations has led to widespread interest among raw material-producing nations to develop cartels or cartel-like arrangements in order to extract higher prices from the consuming nations of the world. The ability of producing nations to sustain an effort to establish higher prices through cartels is limited because of the vast differences among individual nations producing any given commoditiy. There is also a considerable degree of confusion concerning the extent to which interruptions in supply or substantial price manipulations are tactics to which the United States and its allies may be vulnerable. Two recent studies by different organs of the US government illustrate the confusion. A special report entitled *Critical Imported Materials*, by the White House Council on International Economic Policy, states:[33]

> Embargoes of raw materials are highly unlikely. They do not make economic sense in terms of producers' revenue objectives. The objective of increased revenue argues for selling at a high price rather than denying the product altogether. An embargo, however, may be undertaken for political reasons, as in the case of the Arab oil producers . . . The degree of supply restriction

---

[33] Council on International Economic Policy, *Special Report: Critical Imported Materials,* Washington, December 1974, p. 20.

entailed in price gouging or cartel-like action would not have a serious effect on US defenses.

In general, the theme of import substitution as a counter to short-term price maximizing by the raw material producing nations is perceived by CIEP as the most effective response to pressure from the producing countries.[34]

A recent study conducted by the National Academy of Sciences is far less optimistic on the possibility of substitution as a means of offsetting supply restrictions by producing nations. It argues instead for vigorous conservation measures. The report concludes:[35]

> The report of the Panel on Materials Conservation through Technology concludes that technology will not always be capable of closing the growing gaps between rising demands and limited supplies of mineral resources. While technology can do much towards conserving resources, it cannot do everything. There are limits to efficiency, to substitution, and to other technological responses. The panel concludes that the federal government should proclaim and deliberately pursue a national policy of conservation of materials, energy, and environmental resources.

The Character of US and Allied Import Dependence

The United States is conspicuously less dependent upon many critical raw material imports than is Western Europe and Japan. Nevertheless, the United States is heavily dependent on imports for many minerals. The statistics in Table 13 suggest the character of the problem.

With the exception of phosphate rock, the United States must import a third or more of its requirements in every commodity except

---

[34] "High oil prices have created the risk that governments of some countries producing other raw materials may feel themselves under strong pressure to adopt a strategy of short-term revenue maximization for their materials exports. Longer-term concern such as loss of market share, substitutions, and lower revenues could be given lower priority under the pressure of imminent inability to pay for vital imports," *Ibid*, p. 20.
[35] National Academy of Sciences, *Mineral Resources and the Environment*, February 13, 1975.

TABLE 13

US, West European, and Japanese Import Dependence on Selected Raw Materials—1972

	United States		OECD Europe		Japan	
	Import Volume (thousands of tons)	Imports as a percentage of Consumption	Import Volume (thousands of tons)	Imports as a percentage of Consumption	Import Volume (thousands of tons)	Imports as a percentage of Consumption
Aluminum	721	14	285	10	333	23
Bauxite and Alumina	13,389	88	3,726	51	4,996	100
Chromium ore	408	100	970	100	875	100
Copper ore and concentrates	49	17	562	93	2,179	90
Copper	334		1,877		332	
Iron ore and concentrates	36,334	32	75,307	37	111,519	94
Lead ore and concentrates	92	19	356	75	199	76
Lead	222		433		5	
Manganese ore	733	95	3,696	98	2,921	90
Nickel ore and concentrates	21	90	176	89	3,165	100
Nickel	119		64		14	
Phosphate rock	52	(a)	20,514	100	3,040	100
Tin ore and concentrates	4		76		negligible	
Tin	52	100	40	96	32	97
Tungsten ore and concentrates	2.7		21.5		2.4	
Zinc ore and concentrates	231	42	1,561	100	1,115	100
Zinc	484	55	302	61	8	80

(a) Net exporter.

aluminum and copper. Europe and Japan must import more than two thirds of their requirements in every commodity except aluminum, iron ore, and zinc. Japan must import over 90 percent of its domestic requirements for every commodity except aluminum, lead, and zinc. Thus, the developed nations of the West, which are largely allied in a series of political and military alliances, are heavily dependent on critical materials for their present structure of output and prices. The extent to which this dependence becomes a problem for Europe and Japan may turn more directly on the relations of the individual nations themselves with the producing countries than on the relationship between the developed world as a whole and the producing nations.

US and Allied Raw Material Dependence: Commodity Analysis

Since 1972, the United States has substantially increased the rate at which it consumes critical raw materials. Statistics are not available for 1974 consumption at this writing; and the worldwide economic slowdown would undoubtedly be reflected in consumption figures of critical raw materials for that year. On the other hand, the consumption patterns established in the 1972-73 period probably reflect the "normal" consumption patterns for the price structure and income levels prevailing at that period. Worldwide increases in consumption would ultimately have forced prices higher as producers reach full capacity and are required to seek out new sources of raw materials at higher prices. Table 14 below provides a useful comparison of the increased rate of consumption in the 1972-73 period as compared to 1968-73.

As noted earlier, the United States is dependent on imports for virtually all these commodities, frequently at very high levels of dependence. The increased rate of consumption suggests that such dependence would be likely to grow in the absence of substantial price changes that would affect the selection of substitutes.

There are important differences among requirements for certain kinds of critical materials, and it is therefore appropriate to discuss each one individually.

TABLE 14
Apparent US Consumption Trends
(Percent Change)

	1968-73 *Annual Average*	*1972-73*
Aluminum	5.9	18
Bauxite	1.6	8
Chromium	1.1	23
Cobalt	6.3	33
Copper	3.8	7
Iron Ore	1.4	13
Lead	2.6	4
Manganese	1.0	15
Natural Rubber	0.5	14
Nickel	3.4	33
Platinum	3.6	21
Tin	—2.3	9
Titanium Metal	5.2	50[a]
Tungsten	5.8	9
Vanadium	1.5	22
Zinc	2.0	7

[a] Most of the 1972-73 increase in apparent consumption was for strategic stockpiling.
Source: Council on International Economic Policy, *Special Report: Critical Imported Materials,* Washington, December 1974, p. 11.

Aluminum. Recent activities by several important producers of bauxite, the major ore used to produce aluminum, have led to a doubling of the price. But because the cost of ore is only a small fraction of the total cost of producing aluminum (ten percent), larger price movements would be required to influence the economic decision to exploit domestic aluminum-bearing ores such as clays, anorthosite, alunite, and others. Western Europe is far less dependent upon developing countries as a source of aluminum ore than is the United States. Over half of Western Europe's domestic requirements comes from Canada, Australia, South Africa, and Rhodesia. Unlike the United States, both Japan and Western Europe get a substantial amount of their aluminum from Communist countries: 27 percent in the case of Western Europe, and ten percent in the case of Japan. The United States thus has two- to three-year substitution possibilities in the event of politically-directed price manipulation or direct embargoes.

Chromium. The United States imports 70 percent of its current chromium demand. The balance is obtained from strategic stockpile sales (20 percent) and secondary recovery techniques (ten percent). As a consequence, recent US imports tend to understate the extent of dependence. Chromium-bearing ores exist in substantial quantities only in the Soviet Union, South Africa, Rhodesia, and Turkey. As a consequence of the UN-mandated embargo on Rhodesian products, the Soviet Union has been the major supplier of chromium ore to Western Europe, Japan, and the United States. Limited substitution opportunities exist by employing nickel steel or titanium, and in some cases aluminum (in circumstances where chrome alloy stainless steel is now employed). An additional alternative is to procure much larger inventories of chromium ore for both commercial and military requirements.

Platinum. The United States has no indigenous platinum resources of any consequence. The major sources of supply for the United States are South Africa (mostly imported by way of the United Kingdom) and the Soviet Union. It is primarily employed as a catalyst in the petrochemical industry, and there are no low-cost substitutes. Together with chromium, it is one of the few materials for which substitution is a relatively long-term and high-cost endeavor.

Iron Ore. Iron ore is one of the most abundant materials in the earth's crust. The United States produces 70 percent of its domestic requirements, and the balance is imported from Canada, Venezuela, and several other South American countries. Virtually all of the world's iron ore is mined by open pit techniques. As a result, it is susceptible to rapid increases in production as a consequence of attempts to shut off supplies or to raise prices for political reasons.

Nickel. The United States imports approximately two thirds of its nickel requirements. It is an important material in making nickel stainless steel. But there are good substitutes for nickel stainless steel;

and in addition, nickel may be obtained from seabed sources at relatively high prices, an industry that is now in its infancy.

Manganese. Virtually all manganese used in the United States is obtained from imported sources. The primary use of manganese is in steel production as a deoxidizing and desulphurizing agent, and occasionally as an alloying element as well. Large quantities of manganese are available from seabed sources; but US requirements at present are met primarily by imports from Gabon, in West Africa, and Brazil. The United States currently maintains an 18-month inventory of manganese.

Tin. The United States has no domestic tin production. Virtually all imports come from three countries: Malaysia, Thailand, and Bolivia, with Malaysia supplying over 50 percent. Tin is unique among metal imports in that it is the only metal controlled by an international commodity agreement, the International Tin Agreement. The United States is not a signatory to this agreement, but the arrangement specified in the agreement has kept tin prices within agreed-upon limits through joint producer-consumer controls over tin production and consumption. The United States maintains a 44-month inventory of tin in its strategic stockpile, although the strategic stockpile objective is only nine months of peacetime consumption. The International Tin Council, the managing agency for the International Tin Agreement, has recently raised the minimum price of tin (to $2.68 per pound) to avoid a situation where the price might return to its early 1973 level of $1.80. The large stockpile maintained by the United States makes it difficult to exploit US vulnerability in tin.

Zinc. Most zinc imports (about 50 percent of US requirements) come from Canada, although Australia, Mexico, Zaire, and Zambia are major zinc producers as well. Domestic US zinc resources could meet domestic requirements if prices rise sufficiently to make production economically feasible.

Natural Rubber. Although the United States employs synthetic rubber for most of its requirements, natural rubber has unique physical properties which make it preferable to synthetic rubber in many circumstances. All US natural rubber is imported, the bulk from Malaysia and Indonesia. Constraints on foreign deliveries of natural rubber can be offset by an increasing use of synthetic rubber; although such uses will, in many circumstances, be inferior to natural rubber. The US stockpile objective for natural rubber is zero, although a two-and-a-half-month stockpile has been maintained. Larger stockpiles would be helpful to offset constraints on foreign supply.

Other Materials. Other critical materials for which the United States is heavily dependent on imports are titanium, cobalt, mercury, tungsten, lead, columbium, vanadium and fluorspar. With the exception of lead, all of the aforementioned materials have substitutes available or multiple supply sources, making it unlikely that any single supplier would be able to control US access to the material. These materials accounted for less than $200 million in imports in 1973. Alternative materials for each of these commodities exist.

The relative abundance of most critical materials is shown in Table 15 below, and current US imports of major critical materials is shown in Table 16.

The United States is growing increasingly dependent upon foreign sources for critical materials, while allowing its own stockpiles to be depleted. Much of the dependence can be offset in a period of time ranging from a few months to a few years. Larger stockpiles are the most acceptable way of dealing with this problem. Special issues arise from the peculiar character of the dependence of Western Europe and Japan on foreign imported materials. Any stockpiling policy which may be adequate for the United States may not be successful because of the consequences of embargoes or politically-motivated price increases aimed at US allies. Under such circumstances, the support of alliance objectives may require much larger inventories of critical raw materials on the part of both the United States and its allies. Tables 17 and 18 present statistics, based on 1972 data reported by the Council on International Economic Policy, on Western Europe's and Japan's share of raw materials imports. The statistics emphasize how much more dependent our industrialized allies are on imported raw materials than the United States.

TABLE 15
Proved World Reserves of Selected Minerals

More than 100 years:	Columbium
	Potash
	Phosphorus
	Magnesium
51-100 years:	Iron ore
	Chromite
	Nickel
	Vanadium
	Cobalt
	Asbestos
	Molybdenum
26-50 years:	Manganese
	Bauxite
	Platinum
	Titanium
	Antimony
	Sulfur
15-25 years:	Copper
	Lead
	Tin
	Zinc
	Tungsten
	Barite
10-15 years:	Mercury
	Silver

Source: Council on International Economic Policy, *Special Report: Critical Imported Materials,* Washington, December 1974, p. 15.

TABLE 16
US Net Imports of Selected Commodities

	Net Imports 1973 $ Millions	Net Imports as Percentage of 1973[a] Consumption	Major Suppliers 1969-72—Percent
Alumina	209	35	Australia (50), Jamaica (22), Surinam (18)
Bauxite	143	90	Jamaica (54), Surinam (23)
Chromium	63	70	USSR (32), South Africa (30), Turkey (18)
Platinum Group Metals	145	95	UK (39),[b] USSR (32), South Africa (12)
Iron Ore	534	28	Canada (50), Venezuela (31)
Nickel	544	65	Canada (82), Norway (8)
Natural Rubber	347	100	Malaysia (40), Indonesia (39)
Manganese	100	82	Gabon (35), Brazil (33)
Zinc	303	48	Canada (60), Mexico (24)
Tin	215	65	Malaysia (64), Thailand (27)
Titanium	48	29	Japan (73), USSR (19), UK (8)
Cobalt	54	95	Zaire (45), Belgium-Luxembourg (29)[c]
Mercury	12	78	Canada (59), Mexico (17)
Tungsten	27	41	Canada (61), Peru (9)
Lead	27	17	Canada (29), Peru (21), Australia (21), Mexico (17)
Columbium	n.a.	63	Brazil (62), Canada (16)
Vanadium	n.a.	25	South Africa (55), Chile (35)
Fluorspar	52	83	Mexico (77), Spain (12)
Copper	143	5	Canada (31), Peru (27), Chile (22)
Phosphates	.... US net exporter		

[a] In quantity terms. Calculated by dividing net imports by total consumption. In some cases, consumption includes withdrawals from (or additions to) government and/or private stocks.
[b] UK sources for raw materials are South Africa, Canada, and the USSR.
[c] Of Zaire origin.

Source: Council on International Economic Policy, *Special Report: Critical Imported Materials*, Washington, December 1974, p. 24.

TABLE 17

West European Raw Material Imports—Major Suppliers

(Share of Total—1972)

	United States	Canada Australia South Africa and Rhodesia	Developing Countries			Communist Countries	Yugoslavia
			Africa exc. South Africa and Rhodesia	Latin America and Caribbean	Asia[a]		
Aluminum	14	26	13	5	2	27	8
Bauxite/Alumina		51	15	12	1	4	17
Chromium ore and concentrates		33	12	—	9	42	2
Copper ore and concentrates	2	48	6	23	10	2	9
Copper	7	41	21	21	1	7	3
Iron ore and concentrates		20	39	37		4	—
Lead ore and concentrates	4	27	34	28		2	5
Lead	1	65	6	12	1	10	5
Manganese ore and concentrates	3	39	38	15	1	4	—
Nickel ore and concentrates		89	—	1	10		—
Nickel	8	67	2	4	1		—
Phosphate rock[b]	22		53			17	—
Tin		1	18	4	66	11	—
Tungsten ore and concentrates	11	16	4	26	25	11	—
Zinc ore and concentrates	1	65	9	21	2	18	1
Zinc	1	43	15			36	4

— Less than 0.5 percent.
[a] Includes Middle East and Oceania.
[b] Percentage figures do not account for all imports.

TABLE 18

Japanese Raw Material Imports—Major Suppliers

(Share of Total—1972)

	United States	Canada Australia New Zealand South Africa and Rhodesia	OECD Europe	Developing Countries			Communist Countries
				Africa exc. South Africa and Rhodesia	Latin America and Caribbean	Asia[a]	
Aluminum	5	53	1	10	1	10	17
Bauxite/Alumina	1	60	—	—	1	38	12
Chromium ore and concentrates	—	51	1	2	5	29	12
Copper ore and concentrates	2	53	—	—	11	34	—
Copper	10	10	2	57	20	1	—
Iron ore and concentrates	1	48	—	7	21	19	2
Lead ore and concentrates	—	77	—	—	13	10	—
Lead	—	21	10	—	39	23	7
Manganese ore and concentrates	—	54	—	10	3	27	5
Nickel ore and concentrates	—	4	—	—	—	96	—
Nickel	3	36	25	—	—	—	36
Phosphate rock	68	—	—	22	1	9	—
Tin ore and concentrates	—	100	—	—	—	—	—
Tin	—	—	—	—	—	98	—
Tungsten ore and concentrates	—	13	—	—	21	63	4
Zinc ore and concentrates	—	42	—	—	48	10	—
Zinc	—	—	—	1	—	5	93

— Less than 0.5 percent.
[a] Includes Middle East and Oceania.

5

Implementing Economic Warfare

The United States has not employed agricultural exports as a component of economic warfare in any serious manner in peacetime. As a consequence, it lacks the bureaucratic and institutional mechanisms to do so. But we have had considerable experience with similar institutional arrangements that are compatible with the conduct of economic warfare, and this experience could readily be drawn upon.

Two mechanisms would be useful to implement such a policy. The first is to obtain tight control by the federal government over the flow of agricultural exports. There has been substantial pressure in recent years to do this for reasons that are primarily protectionist in nature: to minimize the impact of foreign demand on domestic US prices by restricting exports to a level that would limit price increases to an acceptable level. Until the aftermath of the FY 1972 grain sales to the Soviet Union, there was little serious effort to carry out such a program because of its potential adverse effects on international trade. The impact of the July 1973 embargo on soybean exports—especially in Japan and Europe, which are heavily dependent on US soybeans—was formidable, however, and illustrated the kind of reaction that could be expected from any significant interference with international agricultural trade. But the licensing machinery established under the Export Control Act of 1949 does provide the necessary vehicle for limiting agricultural exports if we should wish to do so.[36] Under this

---

[36] This Act was replaced by the Export Administration Act of 1969, which was extended on August 29, 1972. The purpose of the new Act was to reduce the extent of controls, but the machinery was retained.

51

system, all agricultural exports would be required to obtain a validated export license, in a manner similar to present controls on the export of strategic materials and technology to the Soviet Union.

Routine commercial sales to friendly nations would be routinely approved. But exports to nations with respect to which the United States had a powerful political reason to make sales conditional upon some diplomatic arrangement, could be rigorously controlled. At the same time, this form of control would be far less intrusive than some of the proposals that have been advanced in the wake of the Soviet grain deal, the effect of which would be to make agricultural exporters almost totally subject to government monitoring of their business affairs. In addition, this procedure would transform agricultural commodities into an instrument of both economic and political significance, and United States policymakers would have available an additional tool of diplomatic leverage without major institutional change.

The flexibility of agricultural exports as an instrument of foreign policy could be further enhanced through the creation of a grain reserve that could be used entirely as an instrument of government policy. Under the PL480 program, the United States has relied entirely on commercial surpluses to implement agricultural policy. As a result of increased worldwide demand for agricultural commodities, there has been a dramatic drawdown of reserves; and as a result, PL480 shipments have fallen to one third of 1971 levels.[37]

There are a number of current proposals for establishing a centrally operated world food reserve or an internationally coordinated system of national reserves to cope with food shortages.[38] In general, these schemes are humanitarian in purpose, and are designed to assist in the distribution of existing grain reserves among nations that suffer from natural disasters resulting in significant shortfalls. There has also been

---

[37] Worldwide reserves are almost entirely held by the United States, Canada, Argentina, and Australia. Brown, *loc. cit.,* p. 17.

[38] The case for various schemes has been made in T. Josline, "An International Grain Reserve Policy," in *World Food Security,* Report of the Subcommittee on Foreign Agricultural Policy of the Committee on Agriculture and Forestry, US Senate, November 12, 1973; S. S. Rosenfeld, "The Politics of Food," *Foreign Policy* (Spring 1974), pp. 17-29; R. D. Hansen, "The Politics of Scarcity," in J. W. Howe, ed., *The US and the Developing World, Agenda for Action* (New York: Praeger, 1974), pp. 51-65.

much concern among commercial agricultural interests over the prospect that large grain reserves subject to government control would
become a significant "overhang" on the market, resulting in uncertainty in agricultural prices. To a significant extent, this concern is
justified; high agricultural prices can be as much of a deterrent to
consumption as physical shortages of the products themselves.

A proposal more consistent with the commercial interests of the
agricultural exporting nations would be the establishment of a US
government reserve, carefully partitioned from the domestic market,
that would be employed for both humanitarian and political purposes.
The most important attributes of this system would be the following:

(1) Any commercial sales from this reserve, whether foreign or
    domestic, would be at a price that approximated recent market
    prices at the time of sale.

(2) The food reserve should be accumulated by the government in
    a manner that would minimize the impact of such purchases on
    prices in domestic and foreign markets. This could be accom-
    plished by adding to the reserve only in years when there is a
    significant surplus in domestic agricultural production.

(3) Humanitarian relief would be coordinated with other agricul-
    tural exporting nations; but the reserve would be subject to the
    equally valid claims of US diplomatic interests.

The availability of both the mechanism of control and the resource
of a domestic reserve would make possible the exercise of economic
warfare in agricultural commodities as a routine component of US
diplomacy. Not unlike many dimensions of existing diplomatic practice, the mere existence of the institutional mechanisms would constitute a formidable contribution to the effectiveness of diplomacy
toward countries for which agricultural imports constitute a national
necessity.

The manipulation of agricultural exports for diplomatic advantage
is a short-term instrument, as is the short-term character of raw material supply interruptions. This property of agricultural export manipu-

lation makes it a potentially useful instrument of diplomacy Most serious studies of the potential that raw material-producing nations have for the formation of cartels emphasize their long-term infeasibility as a consequence of the availability of substitutes. Producers individually are able to have a significant short-term impact on consuming nations; but the ability of consuming nations to exploit substitutes minimizes the long-term efficacy of such measures.[39] The willingness to employ the agricultural exports mechanism in such cases would provide an incentive to producing states to engage in less economically wasteful and destructive behavior. It would also provide a concomitant diplomatic response to their efforts to establish a multinational mechanism for interrupting raw material supplies.

---

[39] In the recent past, Jamaica has attempted to obtain higher payments from consumers by raising royalties and requiring local processing of bauxite. Other nations have tried nationalization and the modification of concession terms.

6

Strategic Implications

The addition of a viable potential for economic warfare could be a useful option for US policymakers in the decade ahead. For many years, the notion of US policy as reflecting the "powerlessness of the powerful" has tended to define the limits of policy. In the 1960s, it was argued—only half in jest—that the world's only two superpowers were North Korea and North Vietnam; despite their military provocations against the United States while in a position of stark military vulnerability, they enjoyed political immunity from serious US reprisals.

In fact, this circumstance did illustrate the limited number of policy options currently available to the United States between the extremes of simply absorbing a political or military provocation from minor powers, or alternatively responding with the direct threat or use of force. The exception to this, of course, is in the superpower rivalry between the United States and the Soviet Union, where there is a well-developed theory of graduated political and military response at varying levels of provocation.[40] Much less attention has been devoted to the range of appropriate responses to small and medium-sized powers in a political crisis.

The feasibility of employing agricultural exports for diplomatic ends is by no means the entire answer to the problem of dealing with

---

[40] See, for example, Herman Kahn, *On Escalation, Metaphors and Scenarios*, revised edition (Baltimore: Penguin Books, 1968).

small power provocations, any more than it would be a suitable response to the Soviet Union under many circumstances.

The use of agricultural exports as a vehicle to support diplomatic objectives is symmetric with the practice of the Soviet Union, and also appears to be the intention of raw material-exporting, less-developed countries (LDCs). The Soviet Union has employed trade restrictions against a number of countries, both Communist and non-Communist, including Yugoslavia, Albania, Finland, and Communist China.[41] The LDCs, led by Algeria and the Arab oil-producing states, have emphasized the linkage of exports to diplomatic objectives. The legal advisor of the Kuwait Fund for Arab Economic Development has stated:[42]

> A general prohibition on the use of economic measures for political purposes in the international sphere is still an idealist's dream . . . precluding such states from the use of their economic power in the settlement of political disputes before a general ban is imposed on armaments, and in the absence of an effective collective security system, could not serve the interests of international justice.

The use of exports as a vehicle for supporting political or diplomatic objectives is a short-term instrument useful for dealing with short- to intermediate-term political or diplomatic disputes. The impact of withholding agricultural exports will eventually be to encourage the target nation either to seek alternative sources of foreign supply or to promote indigenous production. Neither objective can be accomplished without cost, but both objectives can be accomplished within a three- to five-year period. The utility of agricultural exports as a potential diplomatic lever results from the fact that the withholding of agricultural exports can impart extremely high costs for a few years. Most disputes that are not of a fundamental character can usually be resolved within this period of time. Hence, agricultural

[41] Klaus Knorr, *Power and Wealth, The Political Economy of International Power* (New York: Basic Books, 1973), pp. 138-156.
[42] Statement of I. F. I. Shihata, "Destination Embargo of Arab Oil: Its Legality Under International Law," quoted in L. Dunn, *Beyond the Open Door, US Policy and Access to Global Resources* (Hudson Institute, HI-2148-DP, December 2, 1974).

exports provide a useful diplomatic instrument for short- to inter-mediate-term policy problems with other nations.

The most important potential application of the agricultural export lever is as a means of bringing influence to bear against the Soviet Union. There are several aspects of Soviet agriculture that tend to enhance the utility of economic warfare:

(1) The Soviet Union has traditionally reacted to periodic shortages in domestic agricultural production by belt-tightening measures. There have been six major shortfalls in Soviet agricultural production over the past 20 years, while the United States has had major agricultural shortfalls only once in every two decades since the Civil War. The remedy of belt-tightening is now less acceptable than it once was in the Soviet Union because of the adverse political impact of inadequate agricultural production on a system of domestic incentives and labor productivity in the industrial sector. As a result, the Soviet Union is likely to maintain a strong preference for importing agricultural products to meet shortfalls.

(2) A major effort is being made by the Soviets to alter the composition of their diets by substituting livestock consumption for food grain consumption. Although Soviet grain consumption nearly equals that of the United States, virtually all grain is consumed directly, whereas US per capita consumption is largely indirect consumption through livestock. Soviet feed grain production is likely to be inadequate to the task for the foreseeable future. The Soviets currently have only two million head of beef cattle. To build up an increasing inventory of beef cattle in the face of fluctuating domestic grain production, imports of US feed grains are likely to be a permanent requirement.

(3) There is evidence from Soviet visible trade statistics for 1974 that the Soviets would be acutely vulnerable to the use of agricultural exports as an element of diplomatic leverage in our foreign policy.

It has hitherto been forecast by the CIA and other Western economic specialists that after many years of running a foreign trade
deficit, the Soviet economy would swing sharply into surplus in its
trading with Western capitalist nations. The most popular estimate
was a surplus of $2 billion in 1974. But according to a more recent
projection,[43] the figure may be as little as $150 million. There are
two alternative theories for this dramatic shortfall in expectations.
One attributes it to a one-third rise in Soviet imports from the West,
underscoring their continued interest in Western credits. A second
emphasizes the inability of the Soviets to sell their extractive products,
particularly oil, on the world market. Oil production in the Soviet
Union has fallen behind planned targets, leaving less oil to sell. And
it was frequently sold to Western buyers at prices that exceeded the
Middle East price, causing many traditional buyers to back away
from the Soviet Union as a supplier.[44] One third of Soviet hard cur-
rency earnings are going to consumer expenditures abroad. This could
be entirely wiped out if funds were required to meet a domestic agricultural emergency, thereby inflicting a serious political burden on the
Soviet leadership. The only offset available to the Soviets remains the
sale of gold. The evidence suggests that the Soviet economy is not
capable of meeting its growth objectives without significant interac-
tion with the developed Western economies.

These circumstances provide some explicit opportunities to affect
Soviet political behavior if the United States chooses to employ the
leverage available as a consequence of its dominance of the agricultural export market. The first is to influence resource allocation within
the Soviet economy. Withholding feed grains from the Soviet Union
would have a major impact on resource allocation if the Soviets sought
to maintain their objective of increasing livestock production. Livestock production imposes very high infrastructure costs in any case.
In addition to the problem of providing adequate feed grain supplies,
there are costly feedlots to develop and maintain, major improvements
to be made in the Soviet system of interfarm marketing, in the rural
road network, and in the marketing and distribution of agricultural

---

[43] Michael Kaser and Zoubek, "Russia Pays Its Way—Just," *Financial Times*, April 25, 1975.
[44] For example, the West German firm Veba, which has been a heavy purchaser of Soviet
natural gas and oil, decided to cease purchases in 1974 due to gaps in delivery and high
prices.

commodities, and substantial bureaucratic changes to support the necessary redirection of Soviet agriculture.

Withholding US agricultural exports would compel a shift in resource allocation by the Soviets. As a result of the inefficiency of Soviet agriculture, a disproportionate share of Soviet resources must be devoted to supporting indigenous food requirements. If the United States withheld agricultural exports from the Soviet Union, the Soviets would be deprived of an opportunity to improve their resource allocation by substituting efficient, low-cost US raw agricultural commodities for inefficient and high-cost Soviet products.

The leverage of US feed grain exports would be magnified if they should be withheld, or at least not augmented, during periods of significant shortfalls within the Soviet Union. Major shortages of feed grain would require drastic shifts in the allocation of resources from other sectors of the economy to the agricultural sector, thereby affecting Soviet industrial and military potential. In this regard, the manipulation of agricultural exports to the Soviet Union is more likely to have a significant impact on resource allocation within the Soviet Union than withholding industrial technology. Commenting on this phenomenon, Professor T. C. Shelling has stated:

> Wheat shipments may have the same effect on military programs as jet engine sales. Wheat shipments may permit the Soviets to keep chemical industries oriented toward munitions rather than fertilizers; jet engine sales may permit (them) to allocate engineering resources to consumer goods rather than jet engines.

This view is reinforced by recent research into the US-Soviet dollar/ruble ratio. According to a CIA study,[45] a ruble can buy somewhat more than a dollar's worth of food; but its value would appear to be much greater in relation to most major industrial products. For example, Holzman cites a ruble as worth $9.09 in the purchase of electrical control apparatus, $8.08 in buying power boilers and steam turbines, and $5.56 in relation to metal-cutting machine tools. The stark difference between exchange ratios for some industrial products

---

[45] Cited by Holzman, *op. cit.*, pp. 665.

and those for agricultural commodities is explained by the fact that
the defense sector receives priority in the allocation of investment and
research over the agricultural and consumer goods sectors. Holzman
concludes:

> An embargo designed to prevent the USSR from reaping large
> gains from trade would do well to concentrate on low dollar/
> ruble ratio commodities.

In addition to the economic implications of the manipulation of
agricultural exports, substantial political costs could be imposed on
the Soviet leadership responsible for shortfalls in agricultural output.[46]
This is particularly true where the Soviet leadership has sought to raise
expectations for substantial improvements in the diet in the near
future. It is not apparent as to what extent Soviet leadership would be
willing to absorb these political costs in order to avoid cutting back
on their armed forces. It may be possible to force such a choice on the
Soviet leadership. This is an option which has not hitherto been exploited by US policymakers.[47] With respect to access to resources, the
threat or use of the agricultural lever provides the most serious diplomatic opportunity for avoiding a confrontation between the developed and underdeveloped nations of the world. The crass threats of
blackmail made by some of the leaders of the raw material-producing
nations of the world has left the major industrial powers with little
to speculate about with respect to solutions other than armed intervention.[48]

Willingness to exploit the agricultural export lever would improve
the bargaining position of the United States *vis-à-vis* raw materials
suppliers who are attempting to improve their terms of trade by

---

[46] It has been widely speculated that the failure of the Soviet harvest in 1963-64 was a
primary cause of Krushchev's fall from power in October 1964.

[47] Dunn, *op. cit.*, disputes the efficacy of the agricultural export "weapon" in relation to
the LDCs (although Soviet vulnerability is conceded), as a consequence of the smaller
requirements of the LDCs relative to the size of the international market for agricultural
products. Even in the case of wealthy LDCs, it is often difficult (on a short-term basis) to
replace an international supplier because of existing contracts, seasonal factors, and limited sources of agricultural surpluses. Over the longer term (one year or more), alternative
arrangements could be made. The Arab oil boycott only lasted from October 7, 1973, to
March 18, 1974. Manipulation of agricultural export deliveries would have been a symmetric short-term response to the oil boycott.

[48] Witness the spate of articles concerning an invasion of the Perisan Gulf to secure oil
resources; many of the most prominent spokesmen for military intervention in a future
international crisis were the most vociferous opponents of US military intervention in
Southeast Asia in the 1960s.

establishing cartel arrangements such as OPEC is attempting. There are limited opportunities for producer nations to raise prices through cartel-like arrangements; and as noted earlier, they would weigh less heavily against the United States than against allied nations. But the opportunities do exist. Eventually, the United States and its allies would be driven to substitutes. But the existence of the agricultural lever would dramatically enhance the ability of the United States to negotiate successfully in order to avoid higher cost alternatives for raw materials imports.[49]

During the 1973-74 Arab oil embargo, the United States was not organized for more than two responses: military intervention or passive acceptance of the short-term costs of the embargo. With appropriate organization, a third alternative would have been available as an instrument of diplomacy—the manipulation of the delivery of agricultural products to the region involved. This diplomatic lever is not only commensurate with the provocation, but also far more likely to achieve success than the establishment of a consumers cartel, as has been favored in some quarters.[49]

It is difficult to overlook the "proxy war" aspect of the 1973 oil embargo. The Soviets were a powerful factor in both its intensity and duration through leverage on their Arab clients acquired by means of diplomatic support and a willingness to supply the Arab states with arms. By having available a mechanism that could have been used against the oil-producing nations participating in the embargo, the United States would have been able to support its objectives in the region without resort to the threat or use of force. There are numerous examples of what can be obtained by these means—from relatively short-term advantages, such as extracting or retaining military basing rights from an otherwise reluctant nation, to inhibiting alliances hostile to the interests of the United States. The willingness to exploit our advantages would almost certainly depend upon the stakes involved. It is unlikely that this weapon would be used with much enthusiasm. But its mere existence could constitute a new force in the arsenal of American diplomacy.

---

[49] "Success" in this context does not require that the OPEC nations be brought to their knees. Rather, success implies an ability to influence the behavior of the marginal OPEC member, and providing US negotiators with a genuine bargaining lever in direct negotiations with the nations involved.

Appendix A

Chronology Of The Arab Oil Embargo[50]

Throughout the late Spring and Summer of 1973, the Arab nations brandished the "oil weapon" with increasing frequency. The "weapon" was alternately described as an embargo directed at consuming states "unfriendly" to the Arab cause or as a production cutback of a more general nature. Whatever the means, there was little doubt that the ends were from the outset intensely political—designed to produce a "satisfactory" outcome to the longstanding Arab-Israeli conflict. At no time prior to the embargo was the curtailment of production as a means of raising prices publicly discussed. When the embargo came, it was in response to political and military concerns; nevertheless, its impact on the price of oil was immediate and dramatic.

The first rattles were from Saudi Arabia (where in April, Sheikh Yamani warned the United States that the SAG would not acquiesce to Aramco's ambitious expansion program unless the United States would alter its "pro-Israeli" stance). On May 3, 1973, King Faisal delivered a similar lecture to Aramco President Jungers, threatening a

[50] Source: Subcommittee on Multinational Corporations of the Committee on Foreign Relations, US Senate, *The US Oil Companies and the Arab Oil Embargo, The International Allocation of Constricted Supplies,* January 27, 1975, pp, 13-17.

curtailment of the rate of production expansion. At the end of May, the same message was sounded by Dr. Pachachi, former Secretary General of OPEC, who proposed a crude production "freeze" to force withdrawal of Israeli forces from the 1967 cease-fire lines.

In Libya, production cutbacks accompanied demands for participation in oil company operations. Quaddafi embargoed Bunker Hunt liftings of Sarir crude at the end of May, prior to "nationalization" of the company on June 11. The Libyan leader justified the action by asserting the US deserved a "good hard slap on its insolent faces." On July 19, Iraq threatened the use of embargoes and nationalizations as a "political" weapon. In anticipation of the Arab foreign ministers meeting in Kuwait, scheduled for September 4, the "oil weapon" became a popular subject for speculation throughout the Arab world, while the thrust of developments within OPEC continued to concentrate on pricing. At its 35th meeting on September 15, OPEC demanded renegotiation of the Teheran Agreement, scheduling the first round for October 8 in Vienna.

Although the Vienna talks began on October 8, they were rapidly overtaken by events in the Middle East following the fighting which erupted on October 7, 1973. Initially, the impact on the petroleum market was curiously muted. There were, however, some significant developments. Iraq nationalized US (Exxon and Mobil) interests in the Basrah Petroleum Company on October 7. Military action curtailed up to two thirds of the two million barrels per day exports from major Eastern Mediterranean pipeline terminals. In Europe, Italy and Spain imposed product export controls while France tightened existing product export controls.

On October 9, Kuwaiti Minister Atiqi responded to pressure from his National Assembly and called for an emergency meeting of Arab oil ministers. While pressure for the use of the oil weapon mounted, Aramco was directed to supply crude oil and products to fuel the Arab war effort. Even though the oil and the products had been contracted for and were destined for other customers, the Saudi office of Aramco informed the shareholders that the request was a "matter of state priority," and that Aramco had "no alternative but to comply." In his first cable on this problem, Jungers told the shareholders that "we can probably expect more of this as time goes on." The first request was for crude oil for Egypt, the second was for crude oil and products for Iraq.

On October 15, Jungers cabled from Saudi Arabia that the Saudis were upset over what they believed to be a major American role in the war on the side of the Israelis. He said that Yamani was unhappy about the remarks of a number of United States government officials, including then Vice President Ford, and that unless there was a major change in the tone of remarks coming from the highest level of the United States government, the companies could expect the imposition of a boycott. Yamani said that the pressure for curtailment came mainly from the Libyans and the Iraqis, but that the effort was also being pushed hard by the Kuwaitis and would, therefore, be very difficult to turn around.

Yamani was designated by his government as the principal Saudi official discussing the Saudi role in imposing an oil embargo and as the Saudi government representative at the oil ministers meeting in Kuwait.

On October 16, the "Gulf" committee of OPEC met in Kuwait. They decided to raise prices by 70 percent unilaterally. The following day, the OPEC ministers convened in the same city and agreed on an immediate five percent production cutback from September production. The communique further warned:

> The same percentage will be applied in each month compared with the previous one, until the Israeli withdrawal is completed from the whole Arab territories occupied in June 1967 and the legal rights of the Palestinian people restored. The conferees are aware that this reduction should not harm any friendly state which assisted or will assist the Arabs actively and materially. Such countries would receive their shares as before the reduction.

In the week following this decision, the Arab states individually imposed a rapidly escalating series of restrictions on the supply of crude oil, briefly summarized in the following chronology:

Date	Country	Production cutback (percent)	Embargoes United States	Netherlands	Other
Oct 18	Saudi Arabia	10			
	Qatar	10			
	Libya	5			
	Abu Dhabi		X		
	Algeria		X[a]		
Oct 19	Libya		X		
Oct 20	Bahrain	5	X		Cancellation of 1971 US Navy base agreement.
	Saudi Arabia		X		
	Algeria	10			
Oct 21	Kuwait	10	X		
	Dubai		X		
	Qatar		X		
	Bahrain		X		
	Algeria			X	
Oct 22	Iraq				Nationalized Royal Dutch Shell interest in BPC.
Oct 23	Kuwait			X	
	Abu Dhabi			X	
Oct 24	Qatar			X	
Oct 25	Oman		X	X	
Oct 30	Libya			X	
	Bahrain			X	
Nov 2	Saudi Arabia			X	

[a] Originally imposed October 6.

By early November, the embargoes and cutbacks were firmly in place. The net impact on crude production was approaching a 20 percent reduction due to the fact that both Saudi Arabia and Kuwait first shut in liftings for the embargoed nations and then applied the cutback percentage. Moreover, the rules of the game laid down by the Arabs (with most following the Saudi level) had been refined. The complete embargo applied to all exports to the United States, but also to Canada, the Bahamas, Trinidad, Netherlands Antilles, Puerto Rico, Guam, and the Netherlands). In a separate action, shipments to South Africa and South Yemen were cut off by the SAG.

As the embargo continued, transshipments to other European destinations via Holland and limited deliveries to Canada for domestic consumption were permitted.

In addition to the "embargoed" nations, the Arabs maintained an
"exempt" or "most favored" list of "friendly" nations, including:
France, Spain, United Kingdom, Jordan, Lebanon, Malaysia, Pakistan, Tunisia, and Egypt. These countries were to receive 100 percent
of their September 1973 supplies, notwithstanding the production cutbacks. Accordingly the remaining "neutral' states were effectively cut
back well over the announced percentages.

On November 4, OAPEC ministers reassembled in Kuwait to coordinate the embargo/cutback. They immediately raised the cutback
to 25 percent, but agreed to include the shut-in volumes for embargoed states in this percentage. This move was designed to raise the
smaller producers to the Saudi Arabian level and to establish a uni-
form calculating procedure.

In addition, the embargo of the US was expanded by all Arab
States to include all indirect shipments as well as direct deliveries to
the American market, including deliveries to refiners supplying US
forces in Bahrain, Italy and Greece. The "most favored" list was expanded to include India and all African states which had broken
diplomatic relations with Israel. The cutback of 25 percent from the
September 1973 levels equated to a 32 percent slash of Aramco's projected November production. Conformity was not complete, however.
Iraq participated in the US and Dutch embargo, but refused to sub-
scribe to the production cutbacks. Both Libya and Algeria publicly
announced cutback formulas different from that announced in Kuwait.
Saudi Arabia subsequently added Brazil to the "most favored" list,
while announcing an embargo against Portugal.

In mid-November, Saudi Arabia and Kuwait announced goals of
well beyond the 51 percent participation level. In Vienna, OPEC made
no progress on pricing issues, delaying the decision until December 22.
Ecuador was admitted to OPEC and Gabon was offered associate
status. The Arab ministers also agreed to exempt on a one-time basis
all the EEC nations (except Holland) from the scheduled five percent

December cutback. The spotlight then shifted to the Arab summit meeting held on November 26-28 in Algiers.

At their summit, the ministers made a number of changes in the use of the oil weapon. Specifically, they decided:

(1) That notwithstanding the embargoes and cutbacks, no producing state would be expected to tolerate reductions of more than 25 percent in petroleum export earnings;

(2) To establish a special ministerial committee to "classify" consuming nations as friendly, neutral, or hostile;

(3) To exempt Japan and the Philippines from the December cutbacks only;

(4) To impose an all-Arab embargo on South Africa, Portugal, and Rhodesia;

(5) To establish an Arab Development Bank for Africa;

(6) To draw up a schedule for production increases to correspond to the various stages of an Israeli withdrawal; and

(7) To compensate nonembargoed European nations for the loss of supplies normally transshipped via Holland.

Following the summit, the Saudi Arabian and Algerian oil ministers made a trip to major European capitals to emphasize Arab demands for Israeli withdrawals, but offering to restore production progressively in response to a staged Israeli pullback. On December 8, the Arab oil ministers again assembled in Kuwait to reaffirm the embargo, but Saudi Arabia postponed its scheduled five percent December cutback until January. The SAG also announced it would not consider restoring production above the September 1973 level, even if the Israelis withdrew immediately.

As December drew to a close, a series of momentous decisions were undertaken by the oil producing nations. On December 21,

Libya banned sales to Caribbean refineries (where production is virtually all for US consumption), thus plugging the major "leak" in the Arab embargo of the US. The 37th OPEC meeting in Teheran opened the following day. Concern for the quantity of supply was rapidly transformed into concern for the cost of supply as OPEC raised posted prices by 130 percent. Leading the drive for a major price hike were the Iranians, flushed with the unprecedented $17/barrel prices received at an NIOC auction the week before. During the week of this announcement, OPEC established a simplified pricing system utilizing Arabian light (34°) as the "marker crude," with standard adjustments for specific gravity, sulfur content, and transportation differentials. Also, the Arabs agreed to relax their production cutbacks from 25 percent to 15 percent effective January 1, 1974.

The embargo on exports to the US and Holland was maintained while Japan, the Philippines, and Belgium were granted perferential status. In the case of Belgium, this gesture was retroactive until December 1, 1973. In addition, certain "friendly" countries were granted additional preferences, permitting them to receive more than their September 1973 imports. This special list included the UK (then being crippled by a coal strike) and several Islamic and African nations.

With this action, the Arabs effectively established four categories of consuming nations:

(1) *"Most favored"*—exports to meet current demand;

(2) *"Preferential"*—receiving September 1973 levels or average of January-September 1973 levels;

(3) *"Neutral"*—receiving remaining production, prorationed on January-September 1973 averages;

(4) *"Embargoed"*—receiving no crude oil or refined products.

The internal politics of the December OPEC meeting were instructive. The Saudi representative, Sheikh Yamani, attempted to hold the line on the price rise, under strict instructions from the King, who was anxious to maintain the "political" tone of the embargo. The Shah, on the other hand, was committed to a spectacular price hike —to $17/barrel or more. A compromise emerged.

In January and February 1974, rumors of an impending end to the Arab embargo against the United States proliferated. Speculation was extremely high prior to an Arab oil ministers meeting scheduled for Tripoli (February 13-14, 1974), which was cancelled at the last moment. The intensive shuttle diplomacy of US Secretary of State Kissinger finally bore fruit in mid-March. The embargo against the United States was lifted by most Arab states on March 18, 1974, but continued against Holland. In addition, Iraq and Libya continued an embargo against the US. The curtailment of US petroleum supplies had lasted exactly five months.

Appendix B

1. *Secretary of State Henry A. Kissinger Before the Ministerial Council of the Organization of Economic Cooperation and Development*, Paris, May 28, 1975.

When free nations join forces for the common good, they can achieve great things.

This organization embodies the legacy and the hope of the Marshall Plan, one of the most creative achievements of international collaboration. The nations represented here have every reason to be proud of the advances which they have achieved for their peoples during the past 30 years. Our progress has fostered global progress. Our success has demonstrated that hope, prosperity, and human dignity are not utopian dreams; they can become practical possibilities for all nations.

But the economic system which we labored so hard to construct is now under stress. The energy crisis of 1973 first dramatized the forces of change which threaten to outrun our capacity for cooperative action. A food crisis, a global recession, and a rate of inflation unprecedented in the postwar period have further strained the structure of international cooperation. At the same time, the poorer nations have increasingly pressed their demands for greater benefits and more participation in the international system.

Economic expansion in the industrial world and economic cooperation with the less-developed countries go hand in hand. Only economic growth can satisfy competing demands for more income and more opportunity within, and among, countries. An expanding world economy is essential for development. It stimulates trade, investment, and technology; it supports necessary bilateral and multilateral aid programs; it assures growing markets for the raw materials, manufactures, and agricultural products of the developing countries; it provides the best framework for accommodation on the difficult and potentially divisive issues of food, energy, raw materials, trade, and investment.

These issues go far beyond economic considerations. Economic stagnation breeds political instability. For the nations of the industrialized world, the economic crisis has posed a threat to much more than our national income. It has threatened the stability of our institutions and the fabric of our cooperation on the range of political and security problems. Governments cannot act with assurance while their economies stagnate and they confront increasing domestic and international pressures over the distribution of economic benefit. In such conditions, the ability to act with purpose—to address either our national or international problems—will falter. If they are to contribute to world security and prosperity, the industrialized nations must be economically strong and politically cohesive.

The Organization for Economic Cooperation and Development (OECD) reminds us of our strengths. It calls attention to the wisdom of our predecessors who saw that we multiply our effectiveness by our cooperation. This organization was originally created to promote cooperation among those few nations which were already most advanced. This is still a worthwhile objective, but today's realities demand that we also increasingly base our policies on the recognition that growth in the industrial world is inextricably linked to our relationship with the rest of the world.

We thus face two important challenges:

• First, the challenge to the *nations of the industrial world* to restore sustained and stable economic growth, so essential to maintain confidence in their institutions.

• A challenge to *all nations* to improve the system of international economic cooperation, and thus provide greater opportunity for the less-developed countries to share both the benefits and responsibilities of a growing world economy.

Growth Among the Industrialized Nations

The industrialized nations are now experiencing the most serious economic crisis since the Great Depression of the 1930s. We see it in widespread recession. We encounter it in the inflation that has become the bane of our societies. We note it in the increasing difficulty of governments to manage their economies and even to control their budgets. We observe it in the declining incentives to investment that many of the industrial democracies are willing to offer.

We see how much all our social and economic objectives depend on the general trend of prosperity. A democratic society thrives on a political and social consensus. The distribution of economic benefit must be broadly accepted as just or as offering opportunity for those who seek it. Otherwise, escalating wage and price demands, lagging work performance, and labor unrest will undermine productivity; and inflation, which destroys growth and shatters hope, will be the arbiter of social priorities. Stagnation magnifies all our difficulties; stable growth enhances our possibilities.

The Finance Ministers, meeting tomorrow, will discuss specific measures to achieve our goal. Secretary (of the Treasury William E.) Simon will then describe in detail the trend of American economic recovery. Today, let me offer some general propositions about our long-term future.

Our first task is to rebuild confidence through decisive, coordinated, and mutually supportive action to promote sustained expansion. We must recognize, especially in the short- and medium-term management of our economies, that the economic policies of our nation can have a profound impact on others. And the United States, because of the size and impact of its economy, has a particular obligation to recognize the magnitude of its responsibility.

In the past, we have kept each other informed on short-term policy measures. In a new departure this past Winter, President Ford consulted with Chancellor (of the Federal Republic of Germany Helmut) Schmidt, Prime Minister (of the United Kingdom Harold) Wilson, President (of France Valery) Giscard d'Estaing, and former Prime

Minister (of Japan Kakuei) Tanaka on our efforts to combat the recession. The major industrial countries need to do so. It will greatly improve the chances of avoiding the sequence of boom and bust experienced these last three years. The United States is prepared to cooperate fully in such efforts.

Second, we must collaborate to sustain the growth of international trade and investment. The great postwar effort to liberalize trade, to lessen barriers to investment, and to maintain free monetary exchanges has nourished our prosperity for over a generation. Trade has consistently expanded at a rate twice that of our domestic economy. We must carry this momentum forward in the OECD by renewing our pledge not to resort to restrictive trade measures to cover deficits resulting from current world economic difficulties. And we must take advantage of the multilateral trade negotiations to lower tariffs and nontariff barriers and improve the world trading system.

Third, as I outlined yesterday in the IEA (International Energy Agency), we must collectively adopt strong national and international policies on energy conservation and the development of alternative energy sources. This is indispensable if we are to lower prices and inhibit the political exploitaton of a scarce resource. We must end, or at least reduce, the vulnerability of our economics to external economic or political manipulation.

Finally, we must develop longer-term growth strategies by systematically addressing some fundamental questions:

• How can the industrial nations bring about the massive capital formation required over the next decade for an adequate rate of growth and for a new quality of life?

• What policies are needed to restore a noninflationary environment without which long-term growth cannot occur?

• How can we encourage the research and development necessary to advance the technology vital to growth and to share it with others?

To begin the search for answers to such questions, I propose that we constitute a special group of distinguished economists both in and out of government. Their purpose should be to identify measures that OECD nations can adopt to assure long-term growth. This group should draw on the projections now being developed within the Economic Policy Committee (of the OECD) and turn them into policy recommendations for the next ministerial meeting.

The importance of our economic cooperation transcends immediate economic utility; it also fosters our sense of community and common interest. If we are to cooperate in times of political and military crisis, we cannot, in calmer periods, afford to be economically weak or disunited or preoccupied with clashing economic interests. The interrelationship of our political, economic, and security interests—which the United States suggested two years ago—is a fact, not a theory.

Moreover, eased relations with the Communist world presuppose the political unity and economic vitality of the industrialized countries. The East's incentive to play a responsible role in the world economy and to improve political relationships with the industrialized nations will be enhanced as its stake in our economic success grows. This has been one of the more hopeful trends of recent years, and it is up to us to assure its continuation.

Cooperation With the Developing Nations

Let me now turn to another crucial issue—the relationship between the industrialized nations and the developing world.

The world's prosperity will depend primarily on the industrialized nations, since we account for 65 perent of the world's output and 70 percent of its trade. But our economic well-being depends on a structure of international cooperation in which the developing countries are, and perceive themselves to be, participants. The new problems of our era—insuring adequate supplies of food, energy, and raw materials—require a world economy that accommodates the interests of developing as well as developed countries.

We in this organization all face the same challenge, and we must face it together. The political evolution and economic growth of the last 30 years have brought about a new diffusion of power. No nation or bloc can dominate any longer. Economic issues are turning into central political issues.

Thus, it has become a central test of statesmanship to insure the orderly reconcilation of conflicting interests and to prevent a slide into political and economic warfare. Misused economic power—as the past two years have borne stark witness—can reverse the trend of worldwide growth and retard progress for everyone. An international system will be stable only so long as its economic benefits are widely shared and its arrangements are perceived as just. The United States and, I am sure, all of us in this room are ready to seek solutions to the problems of international cooperation with imagination and compassion.

But it is evident that others must be ready to follow a similar course. Confrontation and cooperation cannot be carried on simultaneously. International meetings that exhaust themselves in self-indulgent rhetoric or self-righteous propaganda help no one and no cause. We do not consider it constructive to participate in such exercises; we have a clear interest in resisting bloc pressure tactics or attempts to impose solutions through hostility. Such methods are futile and counterproductive. If the terribly complex issues before us are to be resolved through tests of strength, it is not the advanced industrial powers who will pay the highest price. Instead, it will be the poorest and most disadvantaged—those in whose name and for whose benefit these tactics are purportedly used.

It is time to end the theoretical debate over whether we are seeking a new order or improving the existing one. Let us deal in reality, not rhetoric. Let us address the practical, common concerns of all the world's peoples with realism, maturity, mutual understanding, and common sense. The United States welcomes a dialogue in that spirit. We will do all we can to make it succeed.

Simple labels falsify the many real communities of interest which exist—some overlapping, some competitive, some complementary.

One of the striking features of the modern world economy is the diversity of its participants. Among the countries formerly classed as "developing," there have emerged in the last decade new economic powers with a growing capacity to export manufacturers and raw materials. The most successful have fostered investment and growth at home. To these emerging powers have now been added the oil-rich countries. Any nation with a moral claim to world leadership—we as well as the newly wealthy—must contribute to easing the plight of the poorest countries. For who can deny that every economic problem—stagnation, inflation, high energy prices, food shortages—hits them hardest?

Areas for Cooperative Efforts

The United States recognizes the responsibility that accompanies its economic power. We are prepared to do our part, in a spirit of equality, mutual respect, and cooperation. Yesterday (in the IEA), I discussed our proposals for achieving a successful multilateral energy dialogue. Today, let me turn to food, raw materials, and trade and finance. A breakdown of the system in these areas would foster economic chaos and instability. Successful collaboration could usher in a new era of economic advance and human progress.

Food. The global problems in food are a central moral and political challenge. A world order in which tens of millions starve and millions more are undernourished will never be accepted as just. The good harvests expected this year should not make us complacent, for the world's total food requirements continue to grow dramatically. The gap between what developing countries can produce and what they need currently amounts to about 25 million tons. At current rates of production and population growth, that gap is expected to double or triple in 10 years. Unless we act now, the world may face a series of increasingly unmanageable food crises over the next quarter century.

For the short term, food aid will continue to be vital to feed the victims of poverty and natural disaster. It is an international responsibility—to be shared by all financially able countries. The United States has pledged that it will make every effort to provide at least four million tons of food aid annually.

But this will not be enough. A long-term solution to the food problem requires that:

• World food production capacity be greatly increased, especially in the developing countries; and

• An international system of grain reserves be created.

Let me turn to the US proposals in this area.

Fortunately, the less-developed nations which are in greatest need also have the greatest potential for increased production. They possess large quantities of unused water and cultivable land and the greatest possibility for improvement in crop yields. Their success, however, requires vast amounts of capital, new methods of planning and funding, and more effective agricultural policies and practices.

To these ends, the United States supports two new international mechanisms:

• First, the International Fund for Agricultural Development. This fund, proposed by the oil-producing nations, is designed to bring together all nations who are prepared to contribute additional resources, over some agreed base year, to agricultural developments. President Ford has asked me to announce that the United States will participate in the creation of such a fund. We believe its resources should total at least $1,000 million a year.

• The link between funding and effective agricultural development strategies should be provided by a second organization, the Consultative Group on Food Production and Investment, which has already been organized as a result of the World Food Conference. This group —sponsored by the World Bank (International Bank for Reconstruction and Development—IBRD), the UN Development Fund, and the Food and Agriculture Organization—plans its first meeting in July. It should be the central mechanism for cooperation among traditional donors, new donors, and the developing countries.

A crucial element in a long-term food strategy is grain reserves. Short-term fluctuations in food production, due to weather or natural or other catastrophes, cause sharp swings in price and availability of precious grains and cause plagues of starvation. A system of grain reserves would make it possible to alleviate famine in bad years, as well as reduce pressures on supply and markets.

• At the Rome food conference (November 1974), we agreed to negotiate a new international system of nationally-held grain reserves. I recently outlined the suggested principles for such a system, which the United States is prepared to begin negotiating immediately:

• First, total world reserves must be large enough to meet potential shortfalls in food grain production.

• Second, grain exporters and importers should agree on a fair allocation of reserve holdings, taking into account wealth, productive capacity, and volume of trade.

• Third, there should be agreed international rules or guidelines to encourage members to build up reserves in times of good harvest.

• Fourth, each participating country should be free to determine how its reserves will be maintained and what incentives will be provided for their build-up and maintenance.

• Fifth, rules or guidelines should be agreed for the drawdown of reserves, triggered by shortfalls in world production. There must be a clear presumption that all members will make reserves available when needed and, conversely, that reserves will not be released prematurely or excessively, thereby depressing market prices.

• Sixth, in times of shortage the system must assure access to supplies for participating countries.

• Seventh, there must be special provisions to meet the needs of the poorer countries.

• Finally, the system must encourage expanded and liberalized trade in grains.

The United States is prepared to hold an important part of an agreed level of world reserves. If others join us, agreement on the outlines of a reserve system can be achieved before the end of the year.

Raw Materials. A second area of increasing concern is commodities. The time is ripe for a detailed look at problems of commodity trade— for solutions that will benefit producers and consumers alike. The current system is marked by volatile prices, disruption of supplies, investment disputes, and increasing hostility to the private capital investment which remains indispensable for the transfer of resources and management skills.

Thus, consumers as well as producers have an interest in effective arrangements. The consuming nations seek reliable supplies and prices. The producing countries seek reliable and growing export earnings to finance development and an adequate return on investments. All nations share an interest in ending the friction which characterizes the issue of raw materials. The debate is becoming more polarized and has already damaged other efforts for international cooperation. The failure of the preparatory energy conference last month (held April 7-15 in Paris) is but a symptom of the larger problem we now confront. The longer we delay, the more difficult and painful it will be to find solutions.

The United States offers the following suggestions:

• First, we propose that new rules and procedures for access to markets and supplies be negotiated in the multilateral trade negotiations now taking place in Geneva.

• Second, we do not believe that exclusive producers organizations are the best way to solve the commodity problem. In our view, consumers and producers should jointly discuss their problems and possible remedial action. We are prepared to do so. Specifically, we are ready to discuss new arrangements for individual commodities on a case-by-case basis. We have already made proposals for a new International Coffee Agreement. We are ready to discuss other commodities as circumstances warrant.

• Third, I have recently suggested that the World Bank increase its financing of resource investments and explore new ways of combining its financing with private management, skills, technology, and capital.

• Finally, for most less-developed countries the key issue is the need for reliable, long-term stability and growth in export earnings. Proposals have been made to review mechanisms for the stabilization of earnings, notably those of the IMF (International Monetary Fund), to protect the developing countries against excessive fluctuations in their export income. We are prepared to join others in this effort.

Others here will have their own views on how to proceed and on new ways of addressing the concerns of the developing nations. Cooperative action among the industrialized nations will multiply the effectiveness of our individual efforts and will insure that we have a clear understanding of common needs. The United States, therefore, strongly supports the OECD recommendations of a high-level group to study proposals on commodities.

Trade and Finance. The traditional areas of international economic cooperation—trade and finance—remain central elements of the economic structure. We cannot adequately provide for new areas of cooperation unless we first assure that the trading and monetary system is functioning effectively. While the present system has come through the last few years quite well, two problems stand out:

• First, developing countries with large and growing industrial sectors, particularly in East Asia and Latin America, require expanding markets for their manufactured goods. We urge the developing countries to approach the issue with the same attitude. We must all realize that the actual diversity of parties and interests demands a variety of responses, that no single solution can be adequate, and that cooperation among the parties most concerned is the most effective means of addressing common problems.

• Second, the poorest countries are badly in need of additional financial help. They now bear a double burden of higher prices for imported energy, food, fertilizer, and industrial goods and of reduced export earnings due to worldwide recession. We therefore support the creation by 1976 of a special trust fund of up to $2,000 million under the IMF. We have proposed that gold now held by the IMF be supplemented by other contributions—especially from oil producers—and be used to provide resources for half of this total. I hope that the countries of the OECD could put this proposal forward for action at the meetings of the IMF Interim Committee and IMF/IBRD Development Committee two weeks from now.

In short, we propose to base the relationship between developed and developing nations on a spirit of cooperation and good will. We urge the developing countries to approach the issue with the same spirit. We must all realize that the actual diversity of parties and interests demands a variety of responses, that no single solution can be adequate, and that cooperation among the parties most concerned is the most effective means of addressing consumers problems.

The United States welcomes the (OECD) Secretary General's proposal for a comprehensive review of our economic relationships with developing countries. We also support the proposal of the government of Japan for a major study, within the OECD, of the longer-run development of the advanced industrial societies in harmony with the less-developed countries.

It is not often in history that a fundamental challenge is so clearly visible and presents such an opportunity to shape our future. We are summoned to seize the possibilities inherent in the new era which the whole world is now entering. We should be confident and not timid; others are seeking to join in what we have built. Our challenge is to encourage progress and not abstract ideological confrontation. With this attitude we can look forward with optimism to the major international deliberations before us, such as the Seventh Special Session of the UN General Assembly this Fall.

Conclusion

Politically, as well as economically, our era has been shaped by the Industrial Revolution and the progressive economic growth that it brought. Its impact has been rapid, its results prodigious, its effects remarkable. It has created a new age of well-being and helped rapid economic growth, which was confined to Western Europe and the United States a century ago, expand into many parts of the globe.

At home, this economic progress has been an essential underpinning of our democracies. It is the basis of a stable, progressive, and just political and social environment.

The new nations now striving to industrialize have with our help a similar opportunity. We have every reason to expect similar success in working together with them on the new challenges of food, raw materials, and energy. But progress will not happen automatically.

So a great deal depends on our determination and vision. There are not plateaus in the affairs of mankind. What is not a step forward is at best stagnation; more often, it is a pause before retreat. There is no need to be dismayed by the problems we face, for progress implies problems. Circumstances have already provided the nations of the world with a unique perception of their interdependence. The opportunity to write a new and enduring chapter in the story of international cooperation is up to us.

We are prepared to respond to the imperatives we face. We have the awareness, the tools, and the determination. Let us now resolve to build the new era that our times demand.

2. *Secretary of State Henry A. Kissinger Before the World Food Conference*, Rome, November 5, 1974.

We meet to address man's most fundamental need. The threat of famine, the fact of hunger have haunted men and nations throughout history. Our presence here is recognition that this eternal problem has now taken on unprecedented scale and urgency and that it can only be dealt with by concerted worldwide action.

Our challenge goes far deeper than one area of human endeavor or one international conference. We are faced not just with the problem of food but with the accelerating momentum of our interdependence. The world is midway between the end of the Second World War and the beginning of the 21st century. We are stranded between old conceptions of political conduct and a wholly new environment, between the inadequacy of the nation-state and the emerging imperative of global community. In the past 30 years, the world came to assume that a stable economic system and spreading prosperity would continue indefinitely. New nations launched themselves confidently on the path of economic and social development; technical innovation and industrial expansion promised steady improvement in the standard of living of all nations; surpluses of fuel, food, and raw materials were considered a burden rather than a blessing. While poverty and misery still afflicted many parts of the globe, over the long run there was universal hope; the period was fairly characterized as a "revolution of rising expectations." That time has ended. Now there are fundamental questions about our capacity to meet even our most basic needs. In 1972, partly due to bad weather around the globe, world grain production declined for the first time in two decades. We were made ominously conscious of the thin edge between hope and hunger, and of the world's dependence on the surplus production of a few nations. In 1973, first a political embargo and then abruptly raised prices for oil curbed production in the world's factories and farms, and sharply accelerated a global inflation that was already at the margin of government's ability to control. In 1974, the international monetary and trading system continues under mounting stress, not yet able to absorb the accumulated weight of repeated shocks. Its institutions are still struggling to respond. The same interdependence that brought common advance now threatens us with common decline.

We must act now and we must act together to regain control over our shared destiny. Catastrophe when it cannot be foreseen can be blamed on a failure of vision or on forces beyond our control. But the current trend is obvious and the remedy is within our power. If we do not act boldly, disaster will result from a failure of will; moral culpability will be inherent in our foreknowledge.

The political challenge is straightforward. Will the nations of the world cooperate to confront a crisis which is both self-evident and global in nature? Or will each nation or region or bloc see its special advantages as a weapon instead of as a contribution? Will we pool our strengths and progress together, or test our strengths and sink together?

President Ford has instructed me to declare on behalf of the United States: We regard our good fortune and strength in the field of food as a global trust. We recognize the responsibilities we bear by virtue of our extraordinary productivity, our advanced technology, and our tradition of assistance. That is why we proposed this conference. That is why a Secretary of State is giving this address. The United States will make a major effort to match its capacity to the magnitude of the challenge. We are convinced that the collective response will have an important influence on the nature of the world that our children inherit.

As we move toward the next century the nations assembled here must begin to fashion a global conception. For we are irreversibly linked to each other—by interdependent economies and human aspirations, by instant communications and nuclear peril. The contemporary agenda of energy, food, and inflation exceeds the capacity of any single government, or even of a few governments together, to resolve.

All nations—east and west, north and south—are linked to a single economic system. Preoccupation with narrow advantages is doomed. It is bound to lead to sterile confrontations, undermining the international cooperation upon which achievement of national objectives depends. The poorest and weakest nations will suffer most. Discontent and instabilities will be magnified in all countries. New dangers will be posed to recent progress in reducing international tensions. But this need not be our future. There is great opportunity as well as grave danger in the present crisis. Recognition of our condition can disenthrall us from outdated conceptions, from institutional inertia, from sterile rivalries. If we comprehend our reality and act upon it, we can usher in a period of unprecedented advance with consequences far transcending the issues before this conference. We will have built an international system worthy of the capacities and aspiration of mankind.

The Food Challenge

We must begin here with the challenge of food. No social system, ideology, or principle of justice can tolerate a world in which the spiritual and physical potential of hundreds of millions is stunted from elemental hunger or inadequate nutrition. National pride or regional suspicions lose any moral and practical justification if they prevent us from overcoming this scourge.

A generation ago, many farmers were self-sufficient; today fuel, fertilizer, capital, and technology are essential for their economic survival. A generation ago, many nations were self-sufficient; today a good many exporters provide the margin between life and death for many millions.

Thus, food has become a central element of the international economy. A world of energy shortages, rampant inflation, and a weakening trade and monetary system will be a world of food shortages as well. And food shortages, in turn, sabotage growth and accelerate inflation.

The food problem has two levels—first, coping with food emergency, and second, assuring long-term supplies and an adequate standard of nutrition for our growing populations.

During the 1950s and 60s, global food production grew with great consistency. Per capita output expanded even in the food-deficit nations; the world's total output increased by more than half. But at the precise moment when growing populations and rising expectations made a continuation of this trend essential, a dramatic change occurred: during the past three years, world cereal production has fallen; reserves have dropped to the point where significant crop failure can speed a major disaster.

The longer-term picture is, if anything, starker still. Even today, hundreds of millions of people do not eat enough for decent and productive lives. Since increases in production are not evenly distributed, the absolute number of malnourished people is, in fact, probably greater today than ever before except in times of famine. In many parts of the world, 30 to 50 percent of the children die before the age of five, millions of them from malnutrition. Many survive only with permanent damage to their intellectual and physical capacities.

World population is projected to double by the end of the century. It is clear that we must meet the food need that this entails. But it is equally clear that population cannot continue indefinitely to double every generation. At some point we will inevitably exceed the earth's capacity to sustain human life. The near- as well as the long-term challenges of food have three components:

• There is the problem of production in the face of population trends. Maintaining even current inadequate levels of nutrition and food security will require that we produce twice as much food by the end of this century. Adequate nutrition would require 150 percent more food, or a total annual output of three billion tons of grain.

• There is the problem of distribution. Secretary General Marei estimates that at the present rate of growth of 2.5 percent a year, the gap between what the developing countries produce themselves and what they need will rise from 25 million to 85 million tons a year by 1985. For the foreseeable future, food will have to be transferred on a substantial scale from where it is in surplus to where it is in shortage.

• There is the problems of reserves. Protection against the vagaries of weather and disaster urgently requires a food reserve. Our estimate is that as much as 60 million tons over current carryover levels may be required.

In short, we are convinced that the world faces a challenge new in its severity, its pervasiveness, and its global dimension. Our minimum objective of the next quarter century must be to more than double world food production and to improve quality. To meet this objective the United States proposes to this conference a comprehensive program of urgent, cooperative worldwide action on five fronts:

• Increasing the production of food exporters;

- Accelerating the production in developing countries;

- Improving means of food distribution and financing;

- Enhancing food quality;

- Ensuring security against food emergencies.

Let me deal with each of these in turn.

Increased Production by Food Exporters

A handful of countries, through good fortune and technology, can produce more than they need and thus are able to export. Reliance on this production is certain to grow through the next decade and perhaps beyond. Unless we are to doom the world to chronic famine, the major exporting nations must rapidly expand their potential and seek to ensure the dependable long-term growth of their supplies.

They must begin by adjusting their agricultural policies to a new economic reality. For years, these policies were based on the premise that production to full capacity created undesirable surpluses and de-pressed markets, depriving farmers of incentives to invest and produce. It is now abundantly clear that this is not the problem we face; there is no surplus so long as there is an unmet need. In that sense, no real surplus has ever existed. The problem has always been a collective failure to transfer apparent surpluses to areas of shortage. In current and foreseeable conditions, this can surely be accomplished without dampening incentives for production in either area.

The United States has taken sweeping steps to expand its output to the maximum. It already has 167 million acres under grain pro-duction alone, an increase of 23 million acres from two years ago. In an address to the Congress last month, President Ford asked for a greater effort still; he called upon every American farmer to produce to full capacity. He directed the elimination of all restrictive practices which raise food prices; he assured farmers that he will use present authority and seek additional authority to allocate the fuel and fertilizer they require; and he urged the removal of remaining acreage limitations.

These efforts should be matched by all exporting countries. Maximum production will require a substantial increase in investment. The best land, the most accessible water, and the most obvious improvements are already in use. Last year, the United States raised its investment in agriculture by $2.5 billion. The United States government is launching a systematic survey of additional investment requirements and of ways to ensure that they are met.

A comparable effort by other nations is essential. The United States believes that cooperative action among exporting countries is required to stimulate rational planning and the necessary increases in output. We are prepared to join with other major exporters in a common commitment to raise production, to make the necessary investment, and to begin rebuilding reserves for food security. Immediately following the conclusion of this conference, the United States proposes to convene a group of major exporters—an export planning group— to shape a concrete and coordinated program to achieve these goals.

Accelerated Production of Developing Countries

The food exporting nations alone will simply not be able to meet the world's basic needs. Ironically but fortunately, it is the nations with the most rapidly growing food deficits which also possess the greatest capacity for increased production. They have the largest amounts of unused land and water. While they now have 35 percent more land in grain production than the developed nations, they produce 20 percent less on this land. In short, the largest growth in world food production can—and must—take place in the chronic deficit countries.

Yet the gap between supply and demand in these countries is growing, not narrowing. At the current growth rate, the grain supply deficit is estimated to more than triple and reach some 85 million tons by 1985. To cut this gap in half would require accelerating their growth rate from the historically high average of 2.5 percent per annum to 3.5 percent—an increase in the rate of growth of 40 percent.

Two key areas need major emphasis to achieve this minimum goal: new research and new investment.

International and national research programs must be concentrated on the special needs of the chronic food deficit nations and they must be intensified. New technologies must be developed to increase yields and reduce costs, making use of the special features of their labor-intensive, capital-short economies.

On the international plane, we must strengthen and expand the research network linking the less developed countries with research institutions in the industrialized countries and with the existing eight international agricultural research centers. We propose that resources for these centers be more than doubled by 1980. For its part the United States will in the same period triple its own contribution for the international centers, for agricultural research efforts in the less developed countries, and for research by American universities on the agricultural problems of developing nations. The existing Consultative Group on International Agricultural Research can play an important coordinating role in this effort.

The United States is gratified by the progress of two initiatives which we proposed at the Sixth Special Session of the UN General Assembly last April: the International Fertilizer Development Center and the study on the impact of climate change on food supply. The Fertilizer Center opened its doors last month in the United States with funds provided by Canada and the United States, we invite wider participation and pledge its resources to the needs of the developing nations. And an important study on climate and food supply has been taken on by the United Nations World Meteorological Organization.

National as well as international research efforts must be brought to bear. The United States offers to share with developing nations the results of its advanced research. We already have under way a considerable range of promising projects: to increase the protein content of common cereals; to fortify staple foods with inexpensive nutrients; to improve plant fixation of atmospheric nitrogen to reduce the need for costly fertilizers; to develop new low-cost, small-scale tools and machines for the world's millions of small farmers.

We also plan a number of new projects. Next year, our space, agriculture, and weather agencies will test advanced satellite techniques for surveying and forecasting important food crops. We will begin in North America and then broaden the project to other parts of the world. To supplement the WMO study on climate, we have begun our own analysis of the relationship between climatic patterns and crop yields over a statistically significant period. This is a promising and potentially vital contribution to rational planning of global production.

The United States will also make available the results of these projects for other nations.

Finally, President Ford is requesting the National Academy of Sciences, in cooperation with the Department of Agriculture and other governmental agencies, to design a farreaching food and nutrition research program to mobilize America's talent. It is the President's aim to dedicate America's resources and America's scientific talent to finding new solutions, commensurate both with the magnitude of the human need and the wealth of our scientific capacities.

While we can hope for technological breakthroughs, we cannot count on them. There is no substitute for additional investment in chronic food-deficit countries. New irrigation systems, storage and distribution systems, production facilities for fertilizer, pesticide, and seed, and agricultural credit institutions are all urgently needed. Much of this can be stimulated and financed locally. But substantial outside resources will be needed for some time to come.

The United States believes that investment should be concentrated in strategic areas, applying existing, and in some cases very simple, technologies to critical variables in the process of food production. Among these are fertilizer, better storage facilities, and pesticides.

Modern fertilizer is probably the most critical single input for increasing crop yields; it is also the most dependent on new investment. In our view, fertilizer production is an ideal area for collaboration between wealthier and poorer nations, especially combining the technology of the developed countries, the capital and raw materials of the oil producers, and the growing needs of the least developed countries. Existing production capacity is inadequate worldwide; new fertilizer industries should be created, especially in the developing countries, to meet local and regional needs for the long term. This could be done most efficiently on the basis of regional cooperation.

The United States will strongly support such regional efforts. In our investment and assistance programs we will give priority to the building of fertilizer industries and will share our advanced technology.

Another major priority must be to reduce losses from inadequate storage, transport, and pest control. Tragically, as much as 15 percent of a country's food production is often lost after harvesting because of pests that attack grain in substandard storage facilities. Better methods of safe storage must be taught and spread as widely as possible. Existing pesticides must be made more generally available. Many of these techniques are simple and inexpensive; investment in these areas could have a rapid and substantial impact on the world's food supply.

To plan a coherent investment strategy, the United States proposes the immediate formation of a coordinating group for food production and investment. We recommend that the World Bank join with the Food and Agricultural Organization and the UN Development Program to convene such a group this year. It should bring together representatives from both traditional donors and new financial powers, from multilateral agencies and from developing countries, with the following mandate:

• To encourage bilateral and international assistance programs to provide the required external resources.

• To help governments stimulate greater internal resources for agriculture.

• To promote the most effective uses of new investment by the chronic deficit countries.

The United States has long been a major contributor to agricultural development. We intend to expand this contribution. We have reordered our development assistance priorities to place the central emphasis on food and nutrition programs. We have requested an increase of almost $350 million for them in our current budget. This new emphasis will continue for as long as the need exists.

For all these international measures to be effective, governments must reexamine their overall agricultural policies and practices. Outside countries can assist with technology and the transfer of resources; the setting of priorities properly remains the province of national authorities. In far too many countries, farmers have no incentive to make the investment required for increased production because prices are set at unremunerative levels, because credit is unavailable, or because transportation and distribution facilities are inadequate. Just as the exporting countries must adjust their own policies to new realities, so must developing countries give a higher priority for food production in their development budgets and in their tax, credit, and investment policies.

Improving Food Distribution and Financing

While we must urgently produce more food, the problem of its distribution will remain crucial. Even with maximum foreseeable agricultural growth in the developing countries, their food import requirement is likely to amount to some 40 million tons a year in the mid-1980s, or nearly twice the current level.

How is the cost of these imports to be met?

The earnings of the developing countries themselves, of course, remain the principal source. The industrialized nations can make a significant contribution simply by improving access to their markets. With the imminent passage of the trade bill, the United States reaffirms its commitment to institute a system of generalized tariff preferences for the developing nations and to pay special attention to their needs in the coming multilateral trade negotiations.

Nevertheless, an expanded flow of food aid will clearly be necessary. During this fiscal year, the United States will increase its food aid contribution, despite the adverse weather conditions which have affected our crops. The American people have a deep and enduring commitment to help feed the starving and the hungry. We will do everything humanly possible to assure that our future contribution will be responsive to the growing needs.

The responsibility for financing food imports cannot, however, rest with the food exporters alone. Over the next few years in particular, the financing needs of the food-deficit developing countries will simply be too large for either their own limited resources or the traditional food aid donors.

The oil exporters have a special responsibility in this regard. Many of them have income far in excess of that needed to balance their international payments or to finance their economic development. The continuing massive transfer of wealth and the resulting impetus to worldwide inflation have shattered the ability of the developing countries to purchase food, fertilizer, and other goods. And the economic crisis has severely reduced the imports of the industrialized countries from the developing nations.

The United States recommends that the traditional donors and the new financial powers participating in the coordinating group for food production and investment make a major effort to provide the food and funds required. They could form a subcommittee on food financing which, as a first task, would negotiate a minimum global quantity of food for whose transfer to food-deficit developing countries over the next three years they are prepared to find the necessary finances.

I have outlined various measures to expand production, to improve the earning capacity of developing countries, to generate new sources of external assistance. But it is not clear that even these measures will be sufficient to meet the longer-term challenge, particularly if our current estimates of the gap by 1985 and beyond prove to be too conservative.

Therefore, ways must be found to move more of the surplus oil revenue into long-term lending or grants to the poorer countries. The

United States proposes that the development committee, created at the recent session of the Governors of the International Bank and Monetary Fund, be charged with the urgent study of whether existing sources of financing are sufficient to meet the expected import requirements of developing countries. If these sources are not sufficient, new means must be found to supplement them. This must become one of the priority objectives of the countries and institutions that have the major influence in the international monetary system.

Enhancing Food Quality

Supplies alone do not guarantee man's nutritional requirements. Even in developed countries, with ample supplies, serious health problems are caused by the wrong kinds and amounts of food. In developing countries, the problem is magnified. Not only inadequate distribution but also the rising cost of food dooms the poorest and most vulnerable groups—children and mothers—to inferior quality as well as insufficient quantity of food. Even with massive gains in food production, the world could still be haunted by the specter of inadequate nutrition.

First, we must understand the problem better. We know a good deal about the state of global production. But our knowledge of the state of global nutrition is abysmal. Therefore, the United States proposes that a global nutrition surveillance system be established by the World Health Organization, the Food and Agricultural Organization, and the United Nations International Children's Emergency Fund. Particular attention should be devoted to the special needs of mothers and young children and to responding quickly to local emergencies affecting these particularly vulnerable groups. Nutrition surveying is a field with which the United States has considerable experience; we are ready to share our knowledge and techniques.

Second, we need new methods for combating malnutrition. The United States invites the WHO, FAO, and UNICEF to arrange for an internationally coordinated program in applied nutritional research. Such a program should set priorities, identify the best centers for research, and generate the necessary funding. The United States is willing to contribute $5 million to initiate such a program.

Third, we need to act on problems which are already clear. The United States proposes an immediate campaign against two of the most prevalent and blighting effects of malnutrition: Vitamin A blindness and iron deficiency anemia. The former is responsible for well over half of the millions of cases of blindness in less developed countries; the current food shortages will predictably increase this number. Iron deficiency anemia is responsible for low productivity in many parts of the world.

Just as the world has come close to eradicating smallpox, yellow fever, and polio, it can conquer these diseases. There are available new and relatively inexpensive techniques which could have a substantial impact. The United States is ready to cooperate with developing countries and international donors to carry out the necessary programs. We are prepared to contribute $10 million to an international effort.

Finally, we need to reflect our concern for food quality in existing programs. This conference should devote special attention to food aid programs explicitly designed to fight malnutrition among the most vulnerable groups. The United States will increase funding for such programs by at least $50 million this year.

Ensuring Against Food Emergencies

The events of the past few years have brought home the grave vulnerability of mankind to food emergencies caused by crop failures, floods, wars and other disasters. The world has come to depend on a few exporting countries, and particularly the United States, to maintain the necessary reserves. But reserves no longer exist, despite the fact that the United States has removed virtually all of its restrictions on production and our farmers have made an all-out effort to maximize output. A worldwide reserve of as much as 60 million tons of food above present carryover levels may be needed to assure adequate food security.

It is neither prudent nor practical for one or even a few countries to be the world's sole holder of reserves. Nations with a history of radical fluctuations in import requirements have an obligation, both to their own people and to the world community, to participate in a system which shares that responsibilty more widely. And exporting countries can no longer afford to be caught by surprise. They must have advance information to plan production and exports.

We commend FAO Director General Boerma for his initiative in the area of reserves. The United States shares his view that a cooperative multilateral system is essential for greater equity and efficiency. We therefore propose that this conference organize a Reserves Coordinating Group to negotiate a detailed agreement on an international system of nationally-held grain reserves at the earliest possible time. It should include all the major exporters as well as those whose import needs are likely to be greatest. This group's work should be carried out in close cooperation with other international efforts to improve the world trading system.

An International Reserve System should include the following elements:

• Exchange of information on levels of reserve and working stocks, on crop prospects, and on intentions regarding imports or exports;

• Agreement on the size of global reserves required to protect against famine and price fluctuations;

• Sharing of the responsibility for holding reserves;

• Guidelines on the management of national reserves, defining the conditions for adding to reserves and for releasing from them;

• Preference for cooperating countries in the distribution of reserves;

• Procedures for adjustment of targets and settlement of disputes, and measures for dealing with noncompliance.

Agenda For The Future

The challenge before this conference is to translate needs into programs and programs into results. We have no time to lose.

I have set forth a five-point platform for joint action:

• To concert the efforts of the major surplus countries to help meet the global demand;

• To expand the capacity of chronic food deficit developing nations for growth and greater self-sufficiency;

• To transfer resources and food to meet the gaps which remain;

• To improve the quality of food to ensure adequate nutrition;

• To safeguard men and nations from sudden emergencies and the vagaries of weather.

I have outlined the contribution that the United States is prepared to make to national or multilateral programs to achieve each of these goals. And I have proposed three new international groups to strengthen national efforts, coordinate them, and give them global focus:

• The Exporters Planning Group;

• The Food Production and Investment Coordinating Group;

• The Reserves Coordinating Group.

A number of suggestions have been made for a central body to fuse our efforts and provide leadership. The United States is open-minded about such an institution. We strongly believe, however, that whatever the mechanisms, a unified, concerted, and comprehensive approach is an absolute requirement. The American delegation headed by our distinguished Secretary of Agriculture Earl Butz is prepared to begin urgent discussions to implement our proposals. We welcome the suggestions of other nations gathered here. We will work hard and we will work cooperatively.

Conclusion

Nothing more overwhelms the human spirit, or mocks our values and our dreams, then the desperate struggle for sustenance. No tragedy is more wounding than the look of despair in the eyes of a starving child.

Once famine was considered part of the normal cycle of man's existence, a local or at worst a national tragedy. Now our consciousness is global. Our achievements, our expectations, and our moral convictions have made this issue into a universal political concern.

The profound promise of our era is that for the first time we may have the technical capacity to free mankind from the scourge of hunger. Therefore, today we must proclaim a bold objective—that within a decade no child will go to bed hungry, that no family will fear for its next day's bread, and that no human being's future and capacities will be stunted by malnutrition.

Our responsibility is clear.

Let the nations gathered here resolve to confront the challenge; not each other.

Let us agree that the scale and severity of the task require a collaborative effort unprecedented in history.

And let us make global cooperation in food a model for our response to other challenges of an interdependent world—energy, inflation, population, protection of the environment.

William Faulkner expressed the confidence that "man will not merely endure, he will prevail." We live today in a world so complex that even only to endure, man must prevail. Global community is no longer a sentimental ideal but a practical necessity. National purposes, international realities and human needs all summon man to a new test of his capacity and his morality.

We cannot turn back or turn away.

"Human reason," Thomas Mann wrote, "needs only to will more strongly than fate and it is fate."

3. *Secretary of State Henry A. Kissinger Before the 29th Session of the United Nations General Assembly,* New York, September 23, 1974.

Last year, in my first address as Secretary of State, I spoke to this Assembly about American purposes. I said that the United States seeks a comprehensive, institutionalized peace, not an armistice. I asked other nations to join us in moving the world from detente to cooperation, from coexistence to community.

In the year that has passed, some progress has been made in dealing with particular crises. But many fundamental issues persist and new issues threaten the very structure of world stability.

Our deepest problem—going far beyond the items on our agenda— is whether our vision can keep pace with our challenges. Will history recall the 20th century as a time of mounting global conflict or as the beginning of a global conception? Will our age of interdependence spur joint progress or common disaster?

The answer is not yet clear. New realities have not yet overcome old patterns of thought and action. Traditional concepts—of national sovereignty, social struggle, and the relation between the old and the new nations—too often guide our course. And so we have managed but not advanced; we have endured but not prospered; and we have continued the luxury of political contention.

This condition has been dramatized in the brief period since last Fall's regular session. War has ravaged the Middle East and Cyprus.

The technology of nuclear explosives has resumed its dangerous spread. Inflation and the threat of global decline hang over the economies of rich and poor alike.

We cannot permit this trend to continue. Conflict between nations once devastated continents; the struggle between blocs may destroy humanity. Ideologies and doctrines drawn from the last century do not even address, let alone solve, the unprecedented problems of today. As a result, events challenge habits; a gulf grows between rhetoric and reality.

The world has dealt with local conflicts as if they were perpetually manageable. We have permitted too many of the underlying causes to fester unattended, until the parties believed that their only recourse was war. And because each crisis ultimately has been contained we have remained complacent. But tolerance of local conflict tempts world holocaust. We have no guarantee that some local crisis—perhaps the next—will not explode beyond control.

The world has dealt with nuclear weapons as if restraint were automatic. Their very awesomeness has chained these weapons for almost three decades; their sophistication and expense have helped to keep constant for a decade the number of states who possess them. Now—as was quite foreseeable—political inhibitions are in danger of crumbling. Nuclear catastrophe looms more plausible—whether through design or miscalculation, accident, theft, or blackmail.

The world has dealt with the economy as if its constant advance were inexorable. While postwar growth has been uneven and some parts of the world have lagged, our attention was focused on how to increase participation in a general advance. We continue to deal with economic issues on a national, regional, or bloc basis at the precise moment that our interdependence is multiplying. Strains on the fabric and institutions of the world economy threaten to engulf us all in a general depression.

The delicate structure of international cooperation, so laboriously constructed over the last quarter century, can hardly survive—and certainly cannot be strengthened—if it is continually subjected to the shocks of political conflict, war, and economic crisis.

The time has come, then, for the nations assembled here to act together on the recognition that continued reliance on old slogans and traditional rivalries will lead us toward:

• A world where local crises threaten global confrontation, and producer and consumer;

• A world where local crises threaten global confrontation, and where the spreading atom threatens global peril;

• A world of rising costs and dwindling supplies, of growing populations and declining production.

Building a More Cooperative World

There is another course. Last week before this Assembly, President Ford dedicated our country to a cooperative, open approach to build a more secure and more prosperous world. The United States will assume the obligations that our values and strength impose upon us.

But the building of a cooperative world is beyond the grasp of any one nation. An interdependent world requires not merely the resources but the vision and creativity of us all. Nations cannot simultaneously confront and cooperate with one another.

We must recognize that the common interest is the only valid test of the national interest.

It is in the common interest, and thus in the interest of each nation:

• That local conflicts be resolved short of force and their root causes removed by political means;

• That the spread of nuclear technology be achieved without the spread of nuclear weapons;

• That growing economic interdependence lift all nations and not drag them down together.

We will not solve these problems during this session, or any one session, of the General Assembly.

But we must at least begin:

- To remedy problems, not just manage them;

- To shape events, rather than endure them;

- To confront our challenges instead of one another.

The Political Dimension

The urgent political responsibility of our era is to resolve conflicts without war. History is replete with examples of the tragedy that sweeps nations when ancient enmities and the inertia of habit freeze the scope for decision. Equally, history is marked by brief moments when an old order is giving way to a pattern new and unforeseen; these are times of potential disorder and danger but also of opportunity for fresh creation.

We face such a moment today. Together let us face its realities:

First, a certain momentum toward peace has been created—in East-West relations and in certain regional conflicts. It must be maintained. But we are only at the beginning of the process. If we do not continue to advance, we will slip back.

Second, progress in negotiation of difficult issues comes only through patience, perseverance, and recogniton of the tolerable limits of the other side. Peace is a process, not a condition. It can only be reached in steps.

Third, failure to recognize and grasp the attainable will prevent the achievement of the ideal. Attempts to resolve all issues at one time are a certain prescription for stagnation. Progress toward peace can be thwarted by asking too much as surely as by asking too little.

Fourth, the world community can help resolve chronic conflicts, but exaggerated expectations will prevent essential accommodation among the parties. This Assembly can help or hinder the negotiating process. It can seek a scapegoat or a solution. It can offer the parties an excuse to escape reality, or sturdy support in search of a compromise. It can decide on propaganda, or contribute to realistic approaches that are responsive to man's yearning for peace.

Middle East

The Middle East starkly demonstrates these considerations. In the past year, we have witnessed both the fourth Arab-Israeli war in a generation and the hopeful beginnings of a political process toward a lasting and just peace.

We have achieved the respite of a cease-fire and of two disengagement agreements, but the shadow of war remains. The legacy of hatred and suffering, the sense of irreconcilability, have begun to yield—however haltingly—to the process of negotiation. But we still have a long road ahead.

One side seeks the recovery of territory and justice for a displaced people. The other side seeks security and recognition by its neighbors of its legitimacy as a nation. In the end, the common goal of peace surely is broad enough to embrace all these aspirations.

Let us be realistic about what must be done. The art of negotiation is to set goals that can be achieved at a given time and to reach them with determination. Each step forward modifies old perceptions and brings about a new situation that improves the chances of a comprehensive settlement.

Because these principles were followed in the Middle East, agreements have been reached in the past year which many thought impossible. They were achieved, above all, because of the wisdom of the leaders of the Middle East who decided that there had been enough stalemate and war; that more might be gained by testing each other in negotiations than by testing each other on the battlefield.

The members of this body, both collectively and individually, have a solemn responsibility to encourage and support the parties in the Middle East on their present course. We have as well an obligation to give our support to the United Nations peacekeeping forces in the Middle East and elsewhere. The United States applauds their indispensable role, as well as the outstanding contribution of Secretary General Waldheim in the cause of peace.

During the past year, my country has made a major effort to promote peace in the Middle East. President Ford has asked me to reaffirm today that we are determined to press forward with these efforts. We will work closely with the parties and we will cooperate with all interested countries within the framework of the Geneva Conference.

Cyprus

The tormented island of Cyprus is another area where peace requires a spirit of compromise, accommodation, and justice. The United States is convinced that the sovereignty, political independence, and territorial integrity of Cyprus must be maintained. It will be up to the parties to decide on the form of government they believe best suited to the particular conditions of Cyprus. They must reach accommodations on the areas to be administered by the Greek and Turkish Cypriot communities as well as on the conditions under which refugees can return to their homes and reside in safety. Finally, no lasting peace is possible unless provisions are agreed upon which will lead to the timely and phased reduction of armed forces and armaments and other war materiel.

The United States is prepared to play an even more active role than in the past in helping the parties find a solution to the centuries-old problem of Cyprus. We will do all we can, but it is those most directly concerned whose effort is most crucial. Third parties should not be asked to produce miraculous outcomes not anchored in reality. Third parties *can* encourage those directly involved to perceive their broader interests; they can assist in the search for elements of agreement by interpreting each side's views and motives to the other. But no mediator can succeed unless the parties genuinely want mediation and are ready to make the difficult decisions needed for a settlement.

The United States is already making a major contribution to help relieve the human suffering of the people of Cyprus. We urge the international community to continue and, if possible, to increase its own humanitarian relief effort.

Africa

The United States notes with particular satisfaction the continuing process of change in Africa. We welcome the positive demonstration of cooperation between the old rulers and the new free. The United States shares and pledges its support for the aspirations of all Africans to participate in the fruits of freedom and human dignity.

The Nuclear Dimension

The second new dimension on our agenda concerns the problem of nuclear proliferation.

The world has grown so accustomed to the existence of nuclear weapons that it assumes they will never be used. But today, technology is rapidly expanding the number of nuclear weapons in the hands of major powers and threatens to put nuclear explosive technology at the disposal of an increasing number of other countries.

In a world where many nations possess nuclear weapons, dangers would be vastly compounded. It would be infinitely more difficult, if not impossible, to maintain stability among a large number of nuclear powers. Local wars would take on a new dimension. Nuclear weapons would be introduced into regions where political conflict remains intense and the parties consider their vital interests overwhelmingly involved. There would, as well, be a vastly heightened risk of direct involvement of the major nuclear powers.

This problem does not concern one country, one region, or one bloc alone. No nation can be indifferent to the spread of nuclear technology; every nation's security is directly affected.

The challenge before the world is to realize the peaceful benefits of nuclear technology without contributing to the growth of nuclear weapons or to the number of states possessing them.

The Need for Restraint

As a major nuclear power, the United States recognizes its special responsibilty. We realize that we cannot expect others to show restraint if we do not ourselves practice restraint. Together with the Soviet Union we are seeking to negotiate new quantitative and qualitative limitations on strategic arms. Last week, our delegations reconvened in Geneva, and we intend to pursue these negotiations with the seriousness of purpose they deserve. The United States has no higher priority than controlling and reducing the levels of nuclear arms.

Beyond the relations of the nuclear powers to each other lies the need to curb the spread of nuclear explosives. We must take into account that plutonium is an essential ingredient of nuclear explosives and that in the immediate future the amount of plutonium generated by peaceful nuclear reactors will be multiplied many times. Heretofore, the United States and a number of other countries have widely supplied nuclear fuels and other nuclear materials in order to promote the use of nuclear energy for peaceful purposes. This policy cannot continue if it leads to the proliferation of nuclear explosives. Sales of these materials can no longer be treated by anyone as a purely commercial competitve enterprise.

The world community, therefore, must work urgently toward a system of effective international safeguards against the diversion of plutonium or its byproducts. The United States is prepared to join with others in a comprehensive effort.

Program for Nuclear Safeguards

Let us together agree on the practical steps which must be taken to assure the benefits of nuclear energy free of its terrors:

• The United States will shortly offer specific proposals to strengthen safeguards to the other principal supplier countries.

• We shall intensify our efforts to gain the broadest possible acceptance of International Atomic Energy Agency (IAEA) safeguards, to establish practical controls on the transfer of nuclear materials, and to ensure the effectiveness of these procedures.

• The United States will urge the IAEA to draft an international convention for enhancing physical security against theft or diversion of nuclear material. Such a convention should set forth specific standards and techniques for protecting materials while in use, storage, and transfer.

• The Treaty on the Nonproliferation of Nuclear Weapons, which this Assembly has endorsed, warrants continuing support. The treaty contains not only a broad commitment to limit the spread of nuclear explosives, but specific obligations to accept and implement IAEA safeguards and to control the transfer of nuclear materials.

Mr. President, whatever advantages seem to accrue from the acquisition of nuclear explosive technology will prove to be ephemeral. When Pandora's box has been opened, no country will be the beneficiary and all mankind will have lost. This is not inevitable. If we act decisively now, we can still control the future.

The Economic Dimension

Lord Keynes wrote: "The power to become habituated to his surroundings is a marked characteristic of mankind. Very few of us realize with conviction the intensely unusual, unstable, complicated, unreliable, temporary nature of the economic organization."

The economic history of the postwar period has been one of sustained growth—for developing as well as developed nations. The universal expectation of our peoples, the foundation of our political institutions, and the assumption underlying the evolving structure of peace are all based on the belief that this growth will continue.

But will it? The increasingly open and cooperative global economic system that we have come to take for granted is now under unprecedented attack. The world is poised on the brink of a return to the unrestrained economic nationalism which accompanied the collapse of economic order in the 1930s. And should that occur, all would suffer—poor as well as rich, producer as well as consumer.

So let us no longer fear to confront in public the facts which have come to dominate our private discussions and concerns.

Economic Crisis Threatens

The early warning signs of a major eonomic crisis are evident. Rates of inflation unprecedented in the past quarter century are sweeping developing and developed nations alike. The world's financial institutions are staggering under the most massive and rapid movements of reserves in history. And profound questions have arisen about meeting man's most fundamental needs for energy and food.

While the present situation threatens every individual and nation, it is the poor who suffer the most. While the wealthier adjust their living standards, the poor see the hopes of a lifetime collapse around them. While others tighten their belts, the poor starve. While others can hope for a better future, the poor see only despair ahead.

It can be in the interest of no country or group of countries to base policies on a test of strength, for a policy of confrontation would end in disaster for all. Meeting man's basic needs for energy and food and assuring economic growth, while mastering inflation, require international cooperation to an unprecedented degree.

The Energy Problem

Let us apply these principles first to the energy situation.

• Oil producers seek a better life for their peoples and a just return for their diminishing resources.

• The developing nations less well-endowed by nature face the disintegration of the results of decades of striving for development as the result of a price policy over which they have no control.

• The developed nations find the industrial civilization built over centuries in jeopardy.

Both producers and consumers have legitimate claims. The problem is to reconcile them for the common good.

The United States is working closely with several oil producers to help diversify their economies. We have established commissions to facilitate the transfer of technology and to assist with industrialization. We are prepared to accept substantial investments in the United States and we welcome a greater role for the oil producers in the management of international economic institutions.

The investment of surplus oil revenues presents a great challenge. The countries which most need these revenues are generally the least likely to receive them. The world's financial institutions have coped thus far, but ways must be found to assure assistance for those countries most in need of it. And the full brunt of the surplus revenues is yet to come.

Despite our best efforts to meet the oil producers' legitimate needs and to channel their resources into constructive uses, the world cannot sustain even the present level of prices, much less continuing increases. The prices of other commodities will inevitably rise in a never-ending inflationary spiral. Nobody will benefit. The oil producers will be forced to spend more for their own imports. Many nations will not be able to withstand the pace and the poorer could be overwhelmed. The complex, fragile structure of global economic cooperation required to sustain national economic growth stands in danger of being shattered.

The United States will work with other consuming nations on means of conservation and on ways to cushion the impact of massive investments from abroad. The preliminary agreement on a program of solidarity and cooperation signed a few days ago in Brussels by the major consumer countries is an encouraging first step.

But the long-range solution requires a new understanding between consumers and producers. Unlike food prices, the high cost of oil is not the result of economic factors, of an actual shortage of capacity, or of the free play of supply and demand. Rather it is caused by deliberate decisions to restrict production and maintain an artificial price level. We recognize that the producers should have a fair share; the fact remains that the present price level even threatens the economic well-being of producers. Ultimately they depend upon the vitality of the world economy for the security of their markets and their investments. And it cannot be in the interest of any nation to magnify the despair of the least developed who are uniquely vulnerable to exorbitant prices and who have no recourse but to pay. What has gone up by political decision can be reduced by political decision.

Adequate World Food Supplies

Last week, President Ford called upon the oil producers to join with consumers in defining a strategy which will meet the world's long-term need for both energy and food at reasonable prices. He set forth the principles which should guide such a policy. And he announced to this Assembly America's determination to meet our responsibilities to help alleviate another grim reality—world hunger.

At a time of universal concern for justice and in an age of advanced technology, it is intolerable that millions are starving and hundreds of millions remain undernourished.

The magnitude of the long-term problem is clear. At present rates of population growth, world food production must double by the end of this century to maintain even the present inadequate dietary level. And an adequate diet for all would require that we triple world production. If we are true to our principles, we have an obligation to strive for an adequate supply of food to every man, woman, and child in the world. This is a technical possibility, a political necessity, and a moral imperative.

The United States is prepared to join with all nations at the World Food Conference in Rome (November 5-16, 1974) to launch the truly massive effort which is required. We will present a number of specific proposals:

• To help developing nations. They have the lowest yields and the largest amounts of unused land and water; their potential in food production must be made to match their growing need.

• To increase substantially global fertilizer production. We must end once and for all the world's chronic fertilizer shortage.

• To expand international, regional, and national research programs. Scientific and technical resources must be mobilized now to meet the demands of the year 2000 and beyond.

• To rebuild the world's food reserves. Our capacity for dealing with famine must be freed from the vagaries of weather.

• To provide a substantial level of concessionary food aid.

The United States will in the coming year increase the value of our own food aid shipments to countries in need. We make this commitment despite great pressures on our economy and at a time when we are seeking to cut our own government budget, because we realize the dimensions of the tragedy with which we are faced. All of us here have a common obligation to prevent the poorest nations from being overwhelmed and enable them to build the social, economic, and political base for self-sufficiency.

The hopes of every nation for a life of peace and plenty rest on an effective international resolution of the crises of inflation, fuel, and food. We must act now and we must act together.

The Human Dimension

Mr. President, let us never forget that all of our political endeavors are ultimately judged by one standard—to translate our actions into human concerns.

The United States will never be satisfied with a world where man's fears overshadow his hopes. We support the United Nations efforts in the fields of international law and human rights. We approve of the activities of the United Nations in social, economic, and humanitarian realms around the world. The United States considers the United Nations World Population Conference last month, the World Food Conference a month from now, and the continuing Law of the Sea Conference of fundamental importance to our common future.

In coming months, the United States will make specific proposals for the United Nations to initiate: a major international effort to prohibit torture; a concerted campaign to control the disease which afflicts and debilitates over 200 million people in 70 countries—schistosomiasis; and a substantial strengthening of the world's capacity to deal with natural disaster—especially the improvement of the United Nation's Disaster Relief Organization.

Conclusion

Mr. President, we have long lived in a world where the consequences of our failures were manageable—a world where local conflicts were contained, nuclear weapons threatened primarily those nations which possessed them, and the cycle of economic growth and decline seemed principally a national concern.

But this is no longer the case. It is no longer possible to imagine that conflicts, weapons, and recession will not spread.

We must now decide. The problems we face will be with us the greater part of the century. But will they be with us as challenges to be overcome or as adversaries that have vanquished us?

It is easy to agree to yet another set of principles or to actions *other* nations should take. But the needs of the poor will not be met by slogans, the needs of an expanding global economy will not be met by new restrictions, the search for peace cannot be conducted on the basis of confrontation. So each nation must ask what *it* can do, what contribution *it* is finally prepared to make to the common good.

Mr. President, beyond peace, beyond prosperity, lie man's deepest aspirations for a life of dignity and justice. And beyond our pride, beyond our concern for the national purpose we are called upon to serve, there must be a concern for the betterment of the human condition. While we cannot, in the brief span allowed to each of us, undo the accumulated problems of centuries, we dare not do less than try. So let us now get on with our task.

Let us act in the spirit of Thucydides that "the bravest are surely those who have the clearest vision of what is before them, glory and danger alike, and yet notwithstanding go out to meet it."

4. *President Gerald R. Ford Before the 29th Session of the United Nations General Assembly*, New York, September 18, 1974.

In 1946, President Harry Truman welcomed representatives of 55 nations to the first General Assembly of the United Nations. Since then, every American President has had the great honor of addressing this Assembly.

Today, with pleasure and humility, I take my turn in welcoming you, the distinguished representatives of 138 nations.

When I took office, I told the American people that my remarks would be "just a little straight talk among friends." Straight talk is what I propose here today in the first of my addresses to the representatives of the world.

Next week, Secretary of State Henry Kissinger will present in specifics the overall principles which I will outline in my remarks

today. It should be emphatically understood that the Secretary of State has my full support and the unquestioned backing of the American people.

As a party leader in the Congress of the United States, as Vice President, and now as President of the United States of America, I have had the closest working relationship with Secretary of State

Kissinger. I have supported and will continue to endorse his many efforts as Secretary of State and in our National Security Council system to build a world of peace.

Since the United Nations was founded, the world has experienced conflicts and threats to peace, but we have avoided the greatest danger—another world war. Today, we have the opportunity to make the remainder of this century an era of peace and cooperation and economic well-being.

The harsh hostilities which once held great powers in their rigid grasp have now begun to moderate. Many of the crises which dominated past General Assemblies are fortunately behind us. And technological progress holds out the hope that one day all men can achieve a decent life.

Nations too often have had no choice but to be either hammer or anvil, to strike or to be struck. Now we have a new opportunity—to forge, in concert with others, a framework of international cooperation. That is the course the United States has chosen for itself.

On behalf of the American people, I renew these basic pledges to you today.

• We are committed to a pursuit of a more peaceful, stable, and cooperative world. While we are determined never to be bested in a test of strength, we will devote our strength to what is best. And in the nuclear era, there is no rational alternative to accords of mutual restraint between the United States and the Soviet Union, two nations which have the power to destroy mankind.

• We will bolster our partnerships with traditional friends in Europe, Asia, and Latin America to meet new challenges in a rapidly changing world. The maintenance of such relationships underpins rather than undercuts the search for peace.

• We will seek out, we will expand our relations with old adversaries. For example, our new rapport with the People's Republic of China best serves the purposes of each nation and the interests of the entire world.

• We will strive to heal old wounds, reopened in recent conflicts in Cyprus, the Middle East, and in Indochina. Peace cannot be imposed from without, but we will do whatever is within our capacity to help achieve it.

• We rededicate ourselves to the search for justice, equality, and freedom. Recent developments in Africa signal the welcome end of colonialism. Behavior appropriate to an era of dependence must give way to the new responsibilties of an era of interdependence.

No single nation, no single group of nations, no single organization can meet all of the challenges before the community of nations. We must act in concert. Progress toward a better world must come through cooperative efforts across the whole range of bilateral and multilateral relations.

America's revolutionary birth and centuries of experience in adjusting democratic government to changing conditions have made Americans practical as well as idealistic. As idealists, we are proud of our role in the founding of the United Nations and in supporting its many accomplishments. As practical people, we are sometimes impatient at what we see as shortcomings.

In my 25 years as a Member of the Congress of the United States, I learned two basic practical lessons:

First, men of differing political persuasions can find common ground for cooperation. We need not agree on all issues in order to agree on most. Differences of principle, of purpose, of perspective will not disappear. But neither will our mutual problems disappear unless we are determined to find mutually helpful solutions.

Second, a majority must take into account the proper interest of a minority if the decisions of the majority are to be accepted. We who believe in and live by majority rule must always be alert to the danger of the "tyranny of the majority." Majority rule thrives on the habits of accommodation, moderation, and consideration of the interests of others.

A very stark reality has tempered America's actions for decades and must now temper the actions of all nations. Prevention of full-scale warfare in the nuclear age has become everybody's responsibility. Today's regional conflict must not become tomorrow's world disaster. We must assure by every means at our disposal that local crises are quickly contained and resolved.

The challenge before the United Nations is very clear. This organization can place the weight of the world community on the side of world peace. And this organization can provide impartial forces to maintain the peace.

And at this point I wish to pay tribute on behalf of the American people to the 37 members of the United Nations peacekeeping forces who have given their lives in the Middle East and in Cyprus in the past 10 months, and I convey our deepest sympathies to their loved ones.

Let the quality of our response measure up to the magnitude of the challenge that we face. I pledge to you that America will continue to be constructive, innovative, and responsive to the work of this great body.

The nations in this hall are united by a deep concern for peace. We are united as well by our desire to ensure a better life for all people.

Today, the economy of the world is under unprecedented stress. We need new approaches to international cooperation to respond effectively to the problems that we face. Developing and developed countries, market and nonmarket countries—we are all a part of one interdependent economic system.

The food and oil crises demonstrate the extent of our interdependence. Many developing nations need the food surplus of a few developed nations. And many industrialized nations need the oil production of a few developing nations.

Energy is required to produce food and food to produce energy—and both to provide a decent life for everyone. The problems of food and energy can be resolved on the basis of cooperation, or can, I should say, be made unmanageable on the basis of confrontation. Runaway inflation, propelled by food and oil price increases, is an early warning signal to all of us.

Let us not delude ourselves. Failure to cooperate on oil and food and inflation could spell disaster for every nation represented in this room. The United Nations must not and need not allow this to occur. A global strategy for food and energy is urgently required.

The United States believes four principles should guide a global approach:

First, all nations must substantially increase production. Just to maintain the present standards of living the world must almost double its output of food and energy to match the expected increase in the world's population by the end of this century. To meet aspirations for a better life, production will have to expand at a significantly faster rate than population growth.

Second, all nations must seek to achieve a level of prices which not only provides an incentive to producers but which consumers can afford. It should now be clear that the developed nations are not the only countries which demand and receive an adequate return for their goods. But it should also be clear that by confronting consumers with production restrictions, artificial pricing, and the prospect of ultimate bankruptcy, producers will eventually become the victims of their own actions.

Third, all nations must avoid the abuse of man's fundamental needs for the sake of narrow national or bloc advantage. The attempt by any nation to use one commodity for political purposes will inevitably tempt other countries to use their commodities for their own purposes.

Fourth, the nations of the world must assure that the poorest among us are not overwhelmed by rising prices of the imports necessary for their survival. The traditional aid donors and the increasingly wealthy oil producers must join in this effort.

The United States recognizes the special responsibility we bear as the world's largest producer of food. That is why Secretary of State Kissinger proposed from this very podium last year a world food conference to define a global food policy. And that is one reason why we have removed domestic restrictions on food productions in the United States.

It has not been our policy to use food as a political weapon, despite the oil embargo and recent oil prices and production decisions.

It would be tempting for the United States—beset by inflation and soaring energy prices—to turn a deaf ear to external appeals for food assistance, or to respond with internal appeals for export controls. But however difficult our own economic situation, we recognize that the plight of others is worse.

Americans have always responded to human emergencies in the past, and we respond again here today. In response to Secretary General Waldheim's appeal and to help meet the long-term challenge in food, I reiterate: To help developing nations realize their aspirations to grow more of their own food, the United States will substantially increase its assistance to agricultural production programs in other countries.

Next, to ensure that the survival of millions of our fellow men does not depend upon the vagaries of weather, the United States is prepared to join in a worldwide effort to negotiate, establish, and maintain an international system of food reserves. This system will work best if each nation is made responsible for managing the reserves that it will have available.

Finally, to make certain that the more immediate needs for food are met this year, the United States will not only maintain the amount it spends for food shipments to nations in need but it will increase this amount this year.

Thus, the United States is striving to help define and help contribute to a cooperative global policy to meet man's immediate and long-term need for food. We will set forth our comprehensive proposals at the World Food Conference in November.

Now is the time for oil producers to define their conception of a global policy on energy to meet the growing need and to do this without imposing unacceptable burdens on the international monetary and trade system.

A world of economic confrontation cannot be a world of political cooperation. If we fail to satisfy man's fundamental needs for energy and food, we face a threat not just to our aspirations for a better life for all our peoples but to our hopes for a more stable and a more peaceful world. By working together to overcome our common problems, mankind can turn from fear towards hope.

From the time of the founding of the United Nations, America volunteered to help nations in need, frequently as the main benefactor. We were able to do it. We were glad to do it. But as new economic forces alter and reshape today's complex world, no nation can be expected to feed all the world's hungry peoples.

Fortunately, however, many nations are increasingly able to help. And I call on them to join with us as truly united nations in the struggle to produce, to provide more food at lower prices for the hungry and, in general, a better life for the needy of this world.

America will continue to do more than its share. But there are realistic limits to our capacities. There is no limit, however, to our determination to act in concert with other nations to fulfill the vision of the United Nations Charter, to save succeeding generations from the scourge of war, and to promote social progress and better standards, better standards of life in larger freedom.

National Strategy Information Center, Inc.

STRATEGY PAPERS

Edited by Frank N. Trager and William Henderson
With the assistance of Dorothy E. Nicolosi

Food, Foreign Policy, and Raw Materials Cartels by William Schneider, February 1976

Strategic Weapons: An Introduction, by Norman Polmar, October 1975

Soviet Sources of Military Doctrine and Strategy by William F. Scott, July 1975

Detente: Promises and Pitfalls by Gerald L. Steibel, March 1975

Oil, Politics, and Sea Power: The Indian Ocean Vortex by Ian W. A. C. Adie, December 1974

The Soviet Presence in Latin America by James D. Theberge, June 1974

The Horn of Africa by J. Bowyer Bell, Jr., December 1973

Research and Development and the Prospects for International Security by Frederick Seitz and Rodney W. Nichols, December 1973

Raw Material Supply in a Multipolar World by Yuan-li Wu. October 1973

The People's Liberation Army: Communist China's Armed Forces by Angus M. Fraser, August 1973 (Out of print)

Nuclear Weapons and the Atlantic Alliance by Wynfred Joshua, May 1973

How to Think About Arms Control and Disarmament by James E. Dougherty, May 1973

The Military Indoctrination of Soviet Youth by Leon Goure, January 1973 (Out of print)

The Asian Alliance: Japan and United States Policy by Franz Michael and Gaston J. Sigur, October 1972

120

Iran, The Arabian Peninsula, and the Indian Ocean by R. M. Burrel and Alvin J. Cottrell, September 1972 (Out of print)

Soviet Naval Power: *Challenge for the 1970s* by Norman Polmar, April 1972. Revised edition, September 1974

How Can We Negotiate with the Communists? by Gerald L. Steibel, March 1972 (Out of print)

Soviet Political Warfare Techniques, Espionage and Propaganda in the 1970s by Lyman B. Kirkpatrick, Jr., and Howland H. Sargeant, January 1972

The Soviet Presence in the Eastern Mediterranean by Lawrence L. Whetten, September 1971

The Military Un*balance*
Is the U.S. Becoming a Second Class Power? June 1971 (Out of print)

The Future of South Vietnam by Brigadier F. P. Serong, February 1971 (Out of print)

Strategy and National Interests: Reflections for the Future by Bernard Brodie, January 1971 (Out of print)

The Mekong River: A Challenge in Peaceful Development for Southeast Asia by Eugene R. Black, December 1970 (Out of print)

Problems of Strategy in the Pacific and Indian Oceans by George G. Thomson, October 1970

Soviet Penetration into the Middle East by Wynfred Joshua, July 1970. Revised edition, October 1971 (Out of print)

Australian Security Policies and Problems by Justus M. van der Kroef, May 1970 (Out of print)

Detente: Dilemma or Disaster? by Gerald L. Steibel, July 1969 (Out of print)

The Prudent Case for Safeguard by William R. Kintner, June 1969 (Out of print)

AGENDA PAPERS

Edited by Frank N. Trager and William Henderson
With the assistance of Dorothy E. Nicolosi

Seven Tracks to Peace in the Middle East by Frank R. Barnett, April 1975

Arms Treaties with Moscow: Unequal Terms Unevenly Applied? by Donald G. Brennan, April 1975

Toward a US Energy Policy by Klaus Knorr, March 1975

Can We Avert Economic Warfare in Raw Materials? US Agriculture as a Blue Chip by William Schneider, July 1974

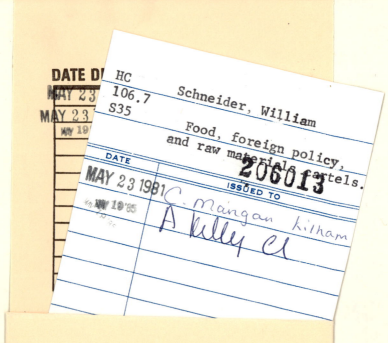